MACHINE AGE MAYA

Machine Age Maya

THE INDUSTRIALIZATION OF A

GUATEMALAN COMMUNITY

MANNING NASH

THE UNIVERSITY OF CHICAGO PRESS

CHICAGO AND LONDON

THE UNIVERSITY OF CHICAGO PRESS
CHICAGO 60637
The University of Chicago Press, Ltd., London

Published 1958

First Phoenix Edition 1967

Third Impression 1973

Printed in the United States of America

ISBN: 0-226-56862-8 (clothbound); 0-226-56863-6 (paperbound)

Library of Congress Catalog Card Number: 67-20810

FOR

ERIC AND LAURA

Preface to the Phoenix Edition

SINCE THE PUBLICATION of this book in 1958 research on the process of industrialization has grown apace.[1] Slotkins' (1960) review covers most of the monographic literature in anthropology and sociology to that date; the work of Moore and Feldman (1960) summarizes the known and unknown aspects of the social consequences of industrialization; in *Industrialization and Society* (1960) Hoseltiz and Moore make a synthesis of the empirical work on industrialization; and several other books codify and order the growing knowledge of social science about industrialization (Kerr et al., 1964; Parsons, 1960; Levy, 1966).

When this book was written the major social science concern about the process of industrialization centered on consequences or impacts. We had before us the historical record of the industrial revolution in Western nations and the single Asian instance of Japan. The historical evidence supported notions of drastic and basic structural transformations as England and other European nations moved from an agriculturally based economy to an industrial one. The few cases or examples in the literature of the spread of the industrial West to Asia and Africa stressed the inherently disruptive consequences of industrialization.

Research published since this book first appeared has given

[1] B. Hoselitz and W. Moore, eds. *Industrialization and Society* (Paris: UNESCO, 1963); C. Kerr *et al., Industrialism and Industrial Man* (New York: Oxford University Press, 1964); Marion J. Levy, Jr., *Modernization and The Structure of Societies. A Setting for International Affairs* (2 Vols.; Princeton, N. J.: Princeton University Press, 1966); W. Moore and A. Feldman, *Labor Commitment and Social Change in Developing Areas* (New York: Social Science Research Council, 1960); T. Parsons, *Structure and Process in Modern Societies* (Glencoe: The Free Press of Glencoe, Ill., 1960); J. Slotkin, *From Field to Factory: New Industrial Employees* (Glencoe: The Free Press of Glencoe, Ill. and University of Chicago, Research Center in Economic Development and Cultural Change, 1960).

a fairly clear picture of the major general consequences of the process of industrialization, both at the local level and at the larger social levels. The major empirical generalizations on the implications of industrialization follow. (Each generalization should be read, the more industrialized the greater the magnitude of the consequential social fact.)

The economy becomes differentiated from other subsystems.

There is an increase in occupational diversity and a tendency toward bureaucratic organization.

Factor markets develop, and labor becomes a factor of production in the market sense. Labor mobility increases.

Corporate kingroups get eroded. Families are moved toward the elemental tasks of socialization of the young and emotional havens for the adults.

Tension between generations increases.

There is a decrease in ascribed statuses beyond the family.

The system of social stratification is class based and performance in the economy is the major index to class position.

In politics there is a rise of a procedural system, a proliferation of administrative bodies, and greater reliance on legal codes.

Politics tends to become participant, and there is a growth of special action structures and voluntary associations.

Religion tends to compete with aggressive nationalism.

Other spheres of action become increasingly separated from religious prescription and proscription.

The divorce of religion from daily life leads to fundamentalist movements.

The expressive and recreational spheres exhibit fads and fashions, and communications networks result in mass culture.

That cities, metropolises, and settlement changes come in the wake of industrialization, along with changes in the age and sex structure of populations and work forces, is also well established by a body of research. The general trends of industrialization, however, leave much room for social variation. And the variations among industrialized societies stem from rather obvious sources: the base culture from which industrialization began; the time of entry into the industrial complex; variations in the ethnic composition of the population undergoing the process;

and, of course, the stream of climactic events such as wars, depressions, and the like.

The empirical generalizations listed above can be cast into diverse theoretical formulations, and a compelling theory from which they can all be deduced without breaks in logic still eludes parsimonious formulation. It is a tribute to social science in general that the work on the consequences of the industrialization process has been as cumulative as it in fact has been.

Around the end of the 1950's it became clear to most scholars in the field of social and cultural change that industrialization was simply the economic component of a larger process of "economic development." [And in turn that economic development was only an aspect of the process of "modernization."] Industrialization came to be viewed as an aspect or stream in the larger process of modernization. Along with this shift in perspective came a change in research emphasis. Scholarly, and indeed practical, concern moved from consequences of industrialization to conditions facilitating economic development.

The decade of the 1950's raised issues like prerequisites to economic development; barriers and obstacles to development; the relative roles of capital and other factors of production in development; and the psychological, social, and cultural conditions favoring or inhibiting development. From this effort vast theoretical schemes emerged. They ranged over psychological variables such as "need for achievement" to a magic formula of "fifteen per cent of gross national product invested annually" makes a society well on the road to development. Like most interesting theories these theoretical structures, largely developed outside of anthropology, usually outran the available facts. It has always been one of social anthropology's major strengths to bring the larger theoretical assertions into contact with ordinary facts of a real society's life in time and space.

Studies like this one are in the first instance an attempt to break down larger generalizations to empirical phrasing and scale. The vast human and social variety in the ethnographic literature serves the anthropologist as a series of ready-made natural "experiments" for the testing of social science generalizations. The methods and concepts of contemporary anthropology are still best suited for the careful, first-hand analysis of a small-scale society. But this sort of analysis, however necessary and useful at this stage of the development of social science, is but a halfway station theoretically. Anthropologists interested in problems like modernization must do two other things, at least, beyond displaying the competence involved in the analysis of a single society. They must work out models for the handling of complex social networks, up to and including the nation, because it is usually a national society that is the relevant ethnological unit in the study of industrialization or modernization. And they must begin to develop their own macro theories, to transcend the comfortable level of the empirical generalization for the icier regions of uncertain theoretical formulation.

If these tasks are undertaken by a substantial number of social anthropologists, the shape and character of anthropological work is bound to alter. Closer multi-disciplinary cooperation is bound to ensue, and a viable general social science may emerge, rather than the parochial disciplinary languages and skills that now characterize social science.

With all of the urgency to treat complex societies and to formulate general theories, it is impossible to forego studies like this one. For in the microanalysis of the interplay of real societies with mental constructs, we are always led to finer formulation, to new questions, and to new images through which we can perceive social reality.

Preface

I AM AWARE that this study is the sort of enterprise anthropologists do not often undertake. Industrialization has been the province of other disciplines in the social sciences. I come to the problem as a consequence of the changing frontiers of anthropological investigation. The problems which face primitives and peasants in their daily lives eventually become the areas of inquiry for anthropology. My interest in the structure and function of small-scale economic systems and the dynamics of economic development comes in part from the common body of anthropological theory and fact. My concern with the industrialization of non-Western peoples stems from this general interest and from the contemporary involvement of much of the world in the attempt to raise economic levels. I take it as a tribute to the vitality and validity of anthropology that my general training and conceptual equipment enabled me to handle the problem of factory impact in Cantel.

I am indebted to the men who taught me anthropology—Sol Tax, Robert Redfield, Fred Eggan, Norman McQuown, and Sherwood Washburn. To Sol Tax I owe a special debt, not only for scholarly guidance and intellectual stimulation, but for his kind personal help and encouragement. To Bert Hoselitz I give thanks for whatever understanding I may have of the problems of economic development and for the opportunity he provided through the Research Center for the Study of Economic Development for the writing up of my field materials.

I cannot find words adequate to describe the magnitude of my indebtedness to my wife, June Nash. Her personal abilities to live in an alien culture helped make our stay in Cantel an adventure, and her professional skills as an anthropologist have contributed heavily to this study. She also drew the maps and illustrations for this text.

During this study I was assisted for two months by Sr. Benjamin

Cush Chan of the Instituto Indigenista de Guatemala. To Sr. Cush and to the ex-director of the Instituto, Joaquin Noval, who provided assistance, I am grateful. To Juan Rosales, now director of the Instituto, I owe thanks for many kindnesses shown me. In Guatemala City, Richard N. Adams offered both scholarly aid and friendship.

I wish to thank the Social Science Research Council, which financed my field work. Publication of this study was aided by the Marian and Adolph Lichtstern fund of the Department of Anthropology, University of Chicago.

To the people of Cantel, and especially to the friends I made there, I take this opportunity to express my appreciation for their cooperation.

I am grateful to Miss Joan Ablon for her help in proof-reading. To Walter Goldschmidt and Betty Bell I owe thanks for editorial guidance, patience, and many suggestions which have improved this work.

Table of Contents

1
Industrialization: An Inquiry into Impacts

THIS is the story of the people of Cantel, an Indian community in the western highlands of Guatemala. It is the description and analysis of a people who have successfully moved from a simple farming technology not much removed from that of their pre-Columbian ancestors, to operating in their midst Central America's largest textile mill.

The adaptation of this Indian community to factory work, cash wages, and the wider ties of the modern industrial world is a precipitate of history. Accommodations between the Indian culture and the factory came through the process of trial and error over more than three generations, without blueprint, without planning agency, and nearly without notice. Today, in the highlands of Guatemala, a people still speaking Quiché, the women yet in costume, the world view of spirits and saints largely intact, have learned how to coexist with a factory regime. Cantel, of course, has changed since the coming of the factory. But the changes, as will be noted later, have been of the kind which permit the people to keep their social integrity and their cultural distinctiveness.

Cantel's experience is the more remarkable when considered in the light of the contemporary spread of industrial technology to peasant and primitive societies. From the Malay archipelago to China, in Africa, in India, the spread of industrial means to overcome poverty has been uniformly subversive of one aspect or another of native society. We have come to think of industrialization as the beginning of a drastic chain of social and cultural change which may some day transform the peasants and primitives of the world into one gray mass of proletarians and level their distinctive and valuable ways of life into one or another pale copy of Western life.

In this image of industrialization, we are hard put to disentangle the complex strands of cause and effect. Even the English experience of transformation, with its wealth of historical documentation, does not clearly inform us as to the impacts we may reasonably expect from factory production, urbanization, religious and scientific reformulation, and moral reinterpretation—all part of that series of events we label the "industrial revolution."

The study of Cantel serves two chief purposes. First, it tells of the way this particular community evolved mechanisms enabling it to adjust to a new mode of production with relatively little cultural loss or social disorganization. Second, Cantel's experience sheds light on the process of industrialization itself, sharpening our insight into social and cultural change, and clarifying our interpretation of cause and effect in any instance of industrial change. These twin theoretical or scientific goals conduce to the practical end at which all science, social included, eventually aims: the conscious and knowledgeable intervention of man in his own affairs.

The burden of making the experience of Cantel scientifically relevant rests in part on the method of study employed and the theoretical apparatus invoked. My way of work has been that of a social anthropologist. And since social anthropology is one of the newer social sciences, I think it necessary to state clearly just what I take social anthropology to be, and how this conception influences my description and analysis of Cantel. Social anthropology depends chiefly upon first-hand, intimate data. The facts about any society are gathered by an anthropologist in the field. My wife and I spent fourteen months in Cantel, living in the town center of the municipio. From our activities of observation, participation, and questioning we built up a picture of Cantel. We attended the principal recurring social activities of marriages, religious processions, funerals, baptisms, markets, and fiestas, as well as observing and taking some part in daily life. We came to know as people and individuals dozens of Cantel men and women. In constructing our picture of the culture of Cantel, we followed the usual field methods of the continual revision of hypothesis as to the meaning of act and artifact. One starts out with some observation or informant's remark on a part of social life. This is data, duly entered in our notebooks or diary, but not yet fact. The social facts we report depend upon thousands of observations, compared over time as to their context, frequency, and meaning. When I say, for example, "the family considers taking a meal together as a nearly sacred occasion," this statement reflects the dozens of meals I have taken with Cantelenses, seeing them keep silent during eating, noticing the formality with which the food is served, hearing accompanying thanks to the deities, and remarking the general attitude of ceremony surrounding the eating. I have also asked them what they think the meal means, and why they do the things they do. And they have told me in part that the meal is akin to the mass, that the food is a token of the beneficence of nature, and that they are thankful to fill their stomachs, and similar kinds of remarks. Each man and woman says something akin to, and yet different from, his fellow villager; just as each meal is like and still different from the one which preceded it and the one which will follow it. My report of the meaning of the meal is a summary of the regularities in meals. It is a blend of things seen and things explained, and becomes a social fact to be reported when I feel that I am able to act in a Cantel meal on the same general premises as do the people of the community. The social anthropologist who follows this procedure works out a culture and society from the experience of living in an alien setting. In different field situations the balance between informant's statement and observation varies. In Cantel, observation much outweighed informant's words, since these people are not given to reflection on the pattern of their lives; and social regularities, the stuff of this study, do not come easily to their lips.

I think the above description makes it plain why anthropologists usually take rather loose research designs to their field of study. That part of a people's life which will come to engage one's time in the field; that special comparison on the spot which may yield new knowledge; those special problems of investigation into sensitive areas; that mine of unsuspected information, all of these ordinary aspects of field work cannot be anticipated. The anthropologist builds his detailed design of investigation in the act of doing field work, since his primary commitment is to the phenomena and their interpretation, not to the gathering of data to fill the slots of some model of social investigation.

In the business of abstracting social regularities from the flow of alien experience, the field worker is continually led into wider and wider areas of observation. To understand a meal in Cantel, some knowledge is necessary of religious organization, kinship relations, agricultural practices, housebuilding, etiquette, and a host of other factors that enter into the preparation, serving, and eating of the meal. Since a field worker cannot know beforehand what is relevant, his procedure is to cast the net of observation as widely as possible, and in the attempt he gets information about all of a people's way of life. From this fact of interconnections between sets of social actions and the exploration of these inter-connections, social anthropology has a dual heritage. Because of their data and their ways of work, social anthropologists are one variety or another of functionalist. They must view the working interdependencies in a people's life in order to bring back even the elementary social and cultural facts. And this data- and method-induced functionalism carries with it the commitment to holism. What is reported is some kind of social whole, seen first hand.

From this microscopic observation of a society, it is expected that macroscopic conclusions will emerge which bear on general questions of man in society. Therefore, in the ideal instance, the field worker does two things. He gathers particular fact and tries to relate it to general conception, to make of his study not only a description and analysis of a single people but to bring it to bear on some general question of scientific importance, or to illuminate some compartment of human nature or social process. Single studies are part of some explicit or implicit framework of comparison, for social anthropology is a comparative discipline. At the minimum, the reported field work takes its place in the growing understanding of the diversities and uniformities of man's social life throughout time and space.

To Cantel we brought some knowledge of the interpretation of industrial impact, both from the writings of our colleagues in anthropology and the kindred social sciences, and from historical analysis. Our task in the field, beyond that of reporting in a meaningful and intelligible manner, was to analyze our data so that they were in some way comparable to other instances of industrialization or technological change. As our image of the community took shape, we decided upon two axes of comparison:

1. The comparison of the factory-employed Indian to the agricultural Indian.
2. The comparison of Cantel as an entire community to surrounding communities, whose difference lay in the absence of the factory.

These axes of comparison in part determine the presentation of the material and exemplify, I believe, one of the arts of social anthropology—the breaking down of the large and abstract quest-ions and generalizations of the social sciences into empirically relev-ant phrasing and scale. Our framework of comparison rests on a particular application of the "method of controlled comparison" as described by Eggan (1954).

When, in the conclusions and summary, I move to those generalizations my data permit, and to some formulation beyond, I commit myself to a kind of explicit theory of social and cultural systems. It is clear that I subscribe to a modified sort of structural and functional theory. The modifications come chiefly from what I have learned about the need for continual accommodation and adaptation in the ordinary life of relatively small societies, and from the importance I place on the consequences of choices people make in attempting these accommodations and adaptations.

It is my conviction that social anthropological procedures are a valuable part of the social sciences. The gathered data, the analyzed whole, the reality of hypothesis, and the broad comparative framework of the discipline give it a distinct place in social investigation. For those who take social science to be the building of fact on fact, Cantel, like other studies, stands as one brick in the growing wall of knowledge about the impact of a factory upon non-Western cultures.

But it is more than that to me, and I think that the more is a regularly recurring feature of anthropological work rather than an idiosyncrasy. Cantel suggests that many of the questions we have been asking about the impact of industrialization, and consequently our conclusions, are far removed from the actual life of a real society in time and space. It leads me to the inference that knowledge about industrialization needs a new armory of questions, a new scheme of imagery, above and beyond the confirming or discarding of existing generalizations about industrialization. The more, then, that I see in Cantel, and in anthropological field study in general, is the transmutation of the guiding questions of inquiry. The new set of problems I can see after my experience in Cantel leads me to say that social anthropology is not only the building of fact on fact and the arrangement of fact into compendent generalization, but a kind of catalyst which continually invokes the re-examination of the whole theoretical apparatus by which we understand human living.

The measure of success of the study of Cantel is twofold: as an understanding of the experience of the people of the community; and as an example which causes us to scrutinize anew our thinking on the consequences of a kind of social change.

2

The Place and the People

CANTEL is one of a series of Indian municipios in the western highlands of Guatemala. Like the other Indian communities (Tax 1937), it is a distinctive social entity. Its physical boundaries are clearly marked. Its inhabitants wear a distinctive costume, and they speak a local variety of Quiché. The customs of its population vary in small but infinite ways from neighboring municipios. It is nearly endogamous. Its people think of themselves as Cantelenses, or Canteleños, people from Cantel who have an ethnic identity and a set of shared understanding which only Cantelenses may have and which sets them apart from the rest of humanity. In common with other highland Indian communities it is part of the rotating marketing system based on its municipio specialization as a corn and wheat exporting center (McBryde 1945). The community carries on its blend of Spanish-Indian culture, more or less stabilized in the area some 400 years ago. The characteristic features are a civil-religious hierarchy, a series of religious brotherhoods devoted to the cult of the saints, a simple small-plot agricultural system at a low level of technological development, and a pecuniary market system (Tax 1953). Witches, spirits, the old 260-day Maya divinatory calendar, mountains with their demons, and personified aspects of nature are part of Cantel's definition of the world.

Cantel's radical difference from other municipios is the presence within its boundaries of Central America's largest cotton textile mill and the employment in that plant of about a fourth of its economically active population.

Studies of other highland Indian communities (Tax 1937, 1953; Wagley 1941, 1949) and some general surveys of the culture of the region (Redfield and Tax 1952) give a fairly detailed and precise idea of the kind of cultural and social patterns common to Mesoamerican Indian communities. These descriptions provide a base line from which some of the changes in Cantel may be charted.

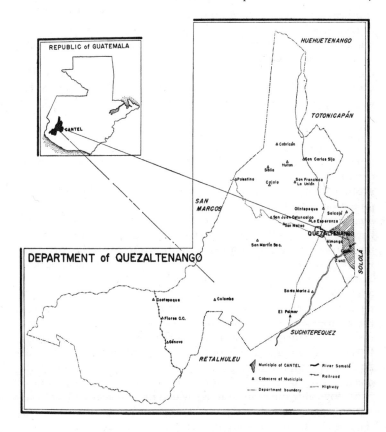

FIG. 1. Department of Quezaltenango.

History, and remembered history as it was obtained from the older Cantelenses, confirms the idea that the general picture drawn by other ethnologists would have described Cantel before the coming of the factory.

Since Cantel is the single case of factory production in the region, and given a reliable base line from which to chart change and known agencies of change, the study of the impact of the factory on Cantel approaches as nearly a "laboratory" situation as the social anthropologist comes upon.

The municipio of Cantel lies more than 200 kilometers west and slightly south of the capital city of Guatemala. It is 12 kilometers southeast of Quezaltenango, the Republic's second city, to which it is connected by an all-weather road (Figure 1). The 26 square kilometers of municipio land lie at the eastern end of the high valley of Quezaltenango. Cantel, which has an average elevation of more than 8,000 feet, sits like an irregular oblong hemmed to the south, east, and west by a belt of young volcanoes. To the north, Cantel opens into the valley.

THE TOWN CENTER

Coming by road from Quezaltenango into Cantel, the land is level. In the town center, a sort of shallow saucer of land, the eye is drawn toward the east by the volcanic mountains which fade into a green and blue haze, and by the Samalá river about a quarter of a mile away, which cuts the Pueblo off from the surrounding rural area. The land drops at a sharp 50 percent grade down to the river, beyond which lies the factory. Across the river is a flat plain where the houses of the rural Cantelenses are scattered in the corn and wheat fields, which also stretch part way up the mountain slopes. To the north the view is interrupted by a large hill, beyond which lies a level stretch. From the town center the eye cannot see the broken terrain, cuts by deep *barrancas* (sheer mountain gorges). To the west the ground rises into a hill, which is capped by the local cemetery. Beyond the cemetery is a short stretch of level agricultural land which falls off into a gorge a mile or so away. The topography puts level land at a premium. One has the feeling of being in a verdant bowl, cracked irregularly and scalloped at the edges with mountains.

Ecologically, the municipio is divided into nuclear and six rural settlements, with trails and paths between the clusters of population (Figure 2). The 1950 census, more reliable than previous censuses, gave the total municipal population as 8,277, with 1,692 in the town center and 6,585 in the remaining settlements (Sexto Censo, 1950:212). If the 1921 census is to be believed, the population of Cantel has increased; the figures for that year are 6,657 for the total, with 1,654 in the town center and 5,003 in the rural areas. The municipio has apparently had a net population gain of only 445 persons since 1893 (Quarto Censo, 1924).

The divisions of the municipio are *cantones*, all farm settlements (the factory and factory housing are in the center of an agricultural settlement), whose names and boundaries are given in Figure 2. The consequences of the settlement pattern are reflected physically, socially, economically, and in the rhythm of life.

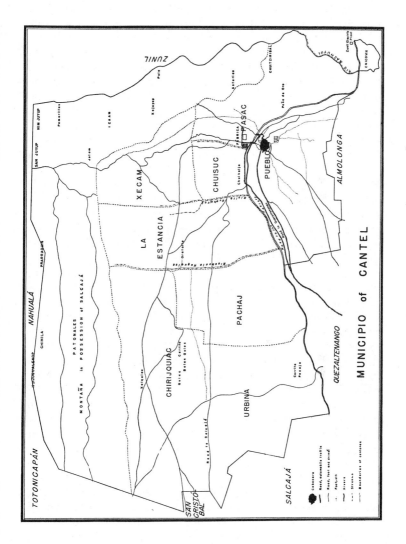

Fig. 2. Municipio of Cantel.

In the Pueblo the houses are tightly crowded in streets which form a grid pattern centering on the plaza square (Figure 3). Only an adobe wall or sometimes a wooden fence separates one house site from another, and the noise, sound, and presence of neighbors is a constant feature. The town center is the social and religious headquarters for the entire municipio. Around the plaza, where the weekly markets are held, are the official buildings. There is the *juzgado*, where the local mayor or *alcalde* holds daily office, the treasurer's office, the headquarters of the chief of police with his 20 local policemen, the separate jails for men and women, and the church where the image of the patron saint resides. All the seven *cofradías*, the religious brotherhoods which care for the saints, have houses in the town center. In addition to being the center of justice and worship, the town attracts the population of the surrounding cantones for fiestas, the Sunday market, the services of the telegraph and post office, the bakeries, the small stores, the electric *molinos*, and the three automobiles which make daily trips to Quezaltenango.

In the town the contiguity of the houses, with fewer than five out of 465 vacant, makes for a frequency and regularity of social intercourse not found in the rural settlements. The clustering of contiguous houses in a limited area, with neighbors who are usually not relatives or even friends, reflects the operation of impersonal factors in the selection of house sites. The town is the chief locus of specialized occupations and stores, and the distribution of houses is a result of the operation of universalistic standards rather than of the particularism of kinship.

The town dweller, if a farmer, leaves his house daily to farm and returns nightly to sleep. He does not need to alternate between town and countryside when he serves in any of the civil or religious offices. The fiestas and the Sunday market are at his doorstep, and even transportation out of town may be obtained in the plaza.

According to our field census, the Pueblo population is 1,910; 96.2 percent are Indians and 3.8 percent are *Ladinos* or non-Indians. The occupational structure of the Pueblo population shows that 17.7 percent of those over 15 years of age are employed in some specialist occupation; when compared to the rural settlement of Estancia where only 11.5 percent are specialists and on a much smaller scale, this indicates that the town center serves as a place for the purchase of services for cash.

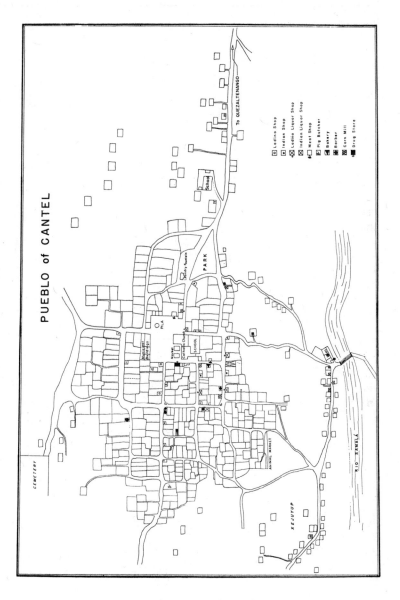

FIG. 3. Pueblo of Cantel.

FIG. 4. Pasac.

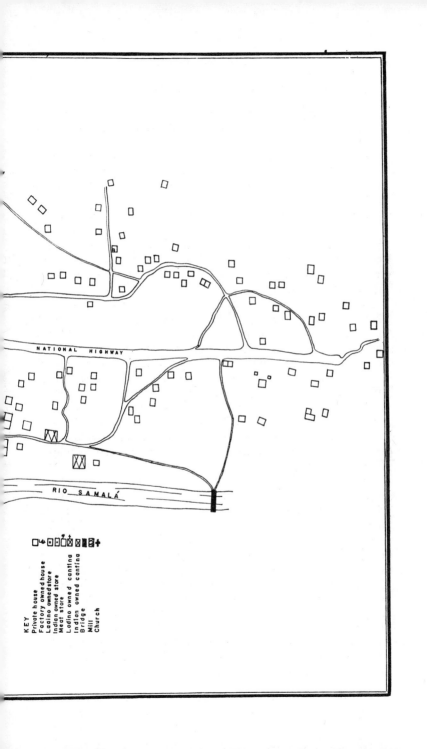

NATIONAL HIGHWAY

RIO SAMALÁ

KEY
Private house
Factory owned house
Ladino owned store
Indian owned store
Meat store
Ladino owned cantina
Indian owned cantina
Bridge
Mill
Church

THE FACTORY SETTLEMENT

Pasac, the nuclear center of houses around the factory, is located where once there was but a settlement of scattered houses; at its core it is now similar to the town in that the houses are ranged along more or less straight streets (Figure 4). House abuts upon house, and privacy is insured by the closed door rather than the adobe wall, since factory housing does not provide a *patio* or open yard.

Because Pasac is a dense settlement of persons many of whom do not own their own houses or house sites and thus cannot pass them on to relatives, there are no clusterings of kinsmen. The cantón is not an administrative center, although it has its separate church, which is subsidiary to the Pueblo church. It has its own patron saints, but no cofradías.

The dominating feature in Pasac is the factory buildings—the plant, storehouse, garage, the unoccupied large house of one of the owners, the special housing for *empleados* (white-collar workers below the policy-making level), the clinic, and the factory school house. Spatial arrangement, residence in a particular house, and rhythm of activity, are largely set by the factory. The factory provides a bus for transportation to Quezaltenango. There is a small market-place on Mondays and on Saturdays, the factory pay day. One large store, formerly factory-owned and now operated by a relative of one of the plant managers, and several small stores combined with homes, give the main thoroughfare a business aspect.

Transportation, stores, and the small market of Pasac make the people less dependent on the town center than are the rural dwellers. The Pasac resident goes to town if a civil or religious office falls to his lot, if he has dealings with the local law, if there is a fiesta, if he wants to buy and sell in the Sunday market, if he has a Catholic ritual to perform in the church, and his children may go to the Pueblo school if he is not a factory employee.

The largest single occupational category in Pasac is factory work; 34 percent of those over fifteen who are economically active are employed in the factory. Only 13.2 percent work at agriculture, but 17.7 percent are engaged in specialists occupations; this is the same percentage as in the town center, but the absolute number and range of services offered is smaller than in the Pueblo. This percentage of specialists reflects the greater demand and ability to pay for cash services on the part of factory workers, when compared to agriculturalists.

Household composition in Pasac is prevalently that of the married pair and their unmarried offspring. Extended forms of the family, either that of married children living with parents or pairs of married siblings in the same household, account for only 19 percent of the households; such extended forms account for 23.7 percent of Pueblo families and 24.9 percent of the censused rural settlement. These percentages of kinds of families, the primary as against the extended, suggest that allocation of housing by the factory has reduced the possibility of forming extended households and that, as will be noted later, there is correspondingly less stress on familial continuity in the factory area.

Pasac has 143 foreign Indians—Indians not born in Cantel—which is the largest number in the entire municipio. Of its 1,823 inhabitants, 87.5 are Indian and 12.5 percent Ladino. This is also the largest percentage of Ladinos in the municipio. The numbers of foreign Indians and Ladinos in Pasac, while not large in proportion to the total population of the municipio, indicate the pulling power of the factory wage for Indians outside of Cantel and for impoverished Ladinos.

THE RURAL CANTONES

The rural areas of Cantel contain most of the population. Judging from surrounding municipios and from an early map of Cantel, these areas presumably show an old and relatively unchanged pattern of settlement and social ecology. We made a complete census and house mapping of the rural canton of Estancia, after sufficient acquaintance with the other rural cantones to realize that it would serve as an example of the others and as a contrast to the town center and to Pasac. In Estancia, as in other rural areas, one house is separated from the next by a stretch of cultivated field, though often a group of four or five houses lie within a small area (Figure 5). There is only one street, called *camino real*. On this street are two stores, the *jefetura* which houses the *alcalde auxiliar* and his aide, the school house, a carpenter shop, several houses, and the gasoline-powered corn mills which the women patronize.

The clustered houses are usually occupied by groups of kinsmen, aggregated areally by the inheritance of land. The related households never function as a group, nor do they form named or corporate bodies.

The economic life of Estancia is reflected in the fact that most men are farmers and most women housewives. Farming does not attract many foreign male Indians or many Ladinos. Of Estancia's 928 persons, 97.6 percent are Indians and only 12 of these were born outside of the municipio.

The other six settlement areas are rural, composed chiefly of farming, indigenous Indians. The agricultural population lives in households scattered upon small plots of land which are usually owned and farmed by the household. There is some clustering of kinsmen, reflecting the inheritance pattern of land, but relatives do not crystallize into kin groupings.

The people of Cantel are Cantelenses or Canteleños. They are people born within the physical area of the municipio, as their forebears were. They are those who may say *ural nitinamit*, "here is my community." They speak a local variety of Quiché which can easily be distinguished from the varieties spoken in nearby Zunil, Almolonga, San Cristóbal, or Totonicapán, for example, although these languages are mutually intelligible. Cantel women are set off from other women in the Quezaltenango valley by small variations in style of dress. Cantel men have a generalized Indian costume which differs from Western male attire in the cut of the suit and the frequent use of a colored band instead of a belt. Their feet are usually bare or sandaled with *caites*.

More important than the distinct social limits of the municipio or the distinctive dress and speech in defining the Cantelenses as a people, is the cultural heritage locally called *nuestra costumbre*. The practice of and the understanding and respect for his particular costumbre distinguishes the Canteleño from all others in the world and, in the end, makes him a member of the tinamit or community. The Canteleños are aware of their cultural distinctiveness, and remark on the funeral practices of Zunil, the marriage customs of Almolonga, the street greeting patterns of San Juan Ostuncalco, for example, as being different—as not constituting costumbre, or the Cantel way of life. Canteleños, then, are a people united by blood and custom, distinct both in their own minds and in fact from their neighbors.

3
The Factory: Its Introduction, History, and Relation to the Community

ESTABLISHING THE FACTORY

IN 1876 the Spanish firm of Sanchez y Hijos brought a cotton textile mill into the municipio of Cantel. The mill was set up along the banks of the Samalá River, because its flow gave enough power to run a turbine, which in turn powered the spinning machines and other machines in the factory. At first the operation was a small one, with 20 cotton spinning machines brought from Oldham, England. The firm built a plant to house its turbine and machines. It employed four English engineers as technical advisors and to show the people they hired "how to work." The land upon which the factory was built, and where it now stands, was in part bought from the municipio and in part from the owner of a small wheat mill, formerly located on the site.

Cantelenses resented the factory. Stories of the fears then current are recited today with a note of mockery. One old man who came to the factory at the age of four, when his parents moved to Cantel from nearby Totonicapán, remembers clearly the voiced fears of the Cantelenses. They thought the factory would swallow up municipal land, wreck costumbre, and drive the people from their municipio. In 1884 this resentment turned into an attempt to oust the factory. The *principales*, or elders of the village, demanded that the factory owners leave the village or the people of Cantel would burn the factory down. In response to this threat, one of the factory's large stockholders, and now a member of the exclusive owning family, appealed to the local *jefe político* and the president of Guatemala for troops. Soldiers of the national army were stationed around the factory and in the town center of Cantel. The presence of troops curbed overt antagonism but the first workers in the factory were not from Cantel, and Cantelenses did not come to the factory in any numbers until about 1890.

Prior to 1880, according to Manuel H., an eighty-one-year-old man who has lived in the factory community since 1878, the factory employed about 25 persons. In 1884 the personnel increased to about 100, and in the 1890's workers ran into the hundreds. Since the turn of the century the work force has fluctuated between 800 and 1,000 persons.

The first workers in the factory were poor, propertyless Ladinos or "Ladinoized" Indians from municipios in the valley, notably Totonicapán, San Cristóbal, Salcajá, Quezaltenango, and San Francisco El Alto. This diversity of origin is still reflected in the non-Cantel element of the factory population. These first workers were furnished land and rent-free houses by the factory, and worked on the half-day shift which characterized the factory schedule until 1884. From the founding of the factory until 1884, wages were no better than a man could make as a full-time field worker or on his own land.

From 1884 to 1890 the factory worked a 12-hour day and had difficulty stabilizing its migrant labor force, and no success in attracting Cantelenses to work. Even in 1890, when the work day was cut to 10 hours, the labor force was characterized by frequent absenteeism, high turnover, and poor work performance.

Around 1890, Canteleños began to come to work in the factory. Manuel H. says they came because they saw that "*no habian novedades*," or that the expected upsets did not occur. From my observations and interviews with workers of many years' employment, it appears that the first Canteleños to seek factory work were of two kinds. They were landless or land-poor men who were pushed by poverty and the inability to find agricultural work, or they were marginal, supplementary, or nonearners in the traditional economic pattern—either children of 8 to 15 or women.

At the turn of the century the factory was firmly entrenched on the banks of the Samalá, working daily, employing hundreds, and operating some 82 machines, with many Canteleños at work in the plant. In 1906 there was some labor trouble. The workers presented demands for higher wages and shorter hours. According to Manuel and other informants, the owners were unable to deal effectively with the worker discontent, but some of the stockholders, a family of four brothers, could and did handle the strike or proposed work stoppage. Their efficient handling of the labor problem resulted in a reorganization of the company; a single family emerged sole owner and remains so to this date. The technique of adjustment in the 1906 dispute was an extension of the method used earlier to deal with the community, except for the use of troops or national police. According to Indian informants involved in early labor disputes, the recipe for labor trouble consisted of calling in the national police to jail the most vocal malcontents, firing individual complainers, and hortatory sermons by the factory managers to those who remained.

Local police were used to offset the chronic absenteeism. They rounded up late or absent workers on Monday mornings and brought them to the factory at the behest of the owners.

Although my data are not full for the period prior to 1945, it is clear that absenteeism, worker discontent, and a fairly extensive turnover were chronic features of the factory until the third or fourth decade of this century. The factory management gradually began to add services and make concessions to the workers which reduced the attrition in the labor force and apparently helped stabilize it. The factory began building houses in 1910, increasing the numbers available to workers until 1945. The main streets of the factory settlement, the public buildings, and many of the factory-owned workers' houses were equipped with electricity in the early 1930's. A clinic was established, and twenty years ago a factory school was opened. Land was loaned to workers without charge. Random interviews with many workers indicate that long, continuous periods of employment are now the rule.

This earlier state of coercion, of bringing in foreigners, of recruiting marginal Cantelenses to work, of low wages and long hours, might be considered a deterrent to the present accommodation of the factory and the community and to the commitment of a Cantel labor force. But just the opposite has in fact obtained. What could easily have been a heritage of suspicion and fear has been converted by the Canteleños, through comparison with the currently better and freer circumstances, into a base line from which to judge present advantage. The first responses of a people to cultural intrusion do not necessarily have the same positive or negative aspect after a time-seasoned judgment.

OPERATING THE FACTORY

In 1954 the factory employed some 900 persons, more than 500 of whom were males; this preserves the established balance of a male-dominated labor force. These people work an eight-hour day, either in the first shift from 6 A.M. to 10 A.M. and 2 P.M. to 6 P.M., or the second shift from 10 A.M. to 2 P.M. and from 6 P.M. to

10 P.M. On Saturdays the work day is from 8 A.M. until noon. They work for cash wages, which in 1954 and for several years prior were set at Q1.20 as the daily minimum (the quetzal, Guatemala's monetary unit, is exactly equivalent to the United States dollar). The work force is divided into several departments—spinning, weaving, dyeing, machine and carpentry shops, and laborers who receive, pack, and unpack cotton and cotton goods. Most of the labor force is employed in spinning cotton into thread and weaving plain cloth. A smaller portion is engaged in using jacquard looms, and a still smaller portion in the dyeing of cloth.

As one enters the factory, the first thing he sees are the machines which take the ginned cotton from the bales and untangle it. In one room are several kinds of spinning machines for making cotton strands. In another room these strands are spun into various weights of thread. The spinning machines are arranged in rows and, depending upon the operation performed and the age and type of machine, an operator runs from two to five machines. The most common arrangement is two or three machines to one operator. For each line of machines there is a *caporal* or foreman, whose job is to see that the machines are fed and running and that the operator is attending them. In another room the weaving machines are arranged similarly to the spinning machines. The dyeing plant is in a separate building. Figure 6 is a diagrammatic presentation of the factory operation, up to the looms.

Like most Latin American factories, each room or section is decorated with a symbol of the faith, a cross with its daily offering of flowers, or with a picture of a saint before which are burning candles. The initial quaint effect of the small brown men and women dressed in picturesque costumes is soon dispelled by the insistent hum of the machines and the coughing induced by the cotton dust. It is a modern factory, run at industrial tempo. The Indian work force fills jobs up to and including the post of caporal and some of the skilled jobs in the machine shop, plant mainten-ance, and electrical and turbine divisions. Ethnic identity as a crit-erion of job fitness begins above those jobs. The engineering skills are still in the hands of foreigners: an English weaving master, English spinning master, and German dyeing master. All of these men are long-time employees of the factory and, together with their foreign wives and families, permanent residents of the factory settlement. Apparently there is some preference for foreign engine-ers, since a Belgian and a Spaniard were hired in 1956 to replace the one deceased and one retired Englishman. The engineers are superior in status to all other technical help and are given an almost free rein in making technical decisions. They do not give orders directly to machine operators, but usually through a native caporal. Outside of the plant they keep aloof from the villagers, who respond with the formal salutations which indicate respect but do not encourage conversation.

The offices of the plant are staffed by Ladinos, who are also resident in the factory housing. These are the white-collar, non-policy-making administrative clerks called empleados. There is a distinct super-subordination relation between the empleados and the *obreros*, the actual factory operators. Although there are Indians competent to fill the post of empleado, none has ever been so employed nor does it seem to be a job for which Indians have ever been considered. Above the empleados is a nephew of the owning family; his is the top administrative post. In practice, important decisions are made by the owning *tios*, the three uncles of the resident administrator. The resident manager functions mainly as a communication channel to the absentee owners, who live in Guatemala City. The day to day administrative detail is carried on by the salaried employees, the chief of whom is called the *administrador*, ostensibly under the guidance of the owners' nephew.

The firm that operates the factory has a deep vertical organization. It does not grow all or even a major part of the cotton consumed, but it does all its own ginning, transports ginned cotton to the mill in its own trucks, and distributes finished goods through its own retail and wholesale outlets or through franchised agencies. Horizontally, it is widespread. Thread, four varieties of undyed cloth, tablecloths, napkins, bedspreads, several patterns of dyed cloth, and several weights and kinds of dyed cloth are manufactured in the one plant. The semimonopolistic position of the mill (it produces nearly seventy percent of the cotton goods purchased in Guatemala) in regard to lack of internal competitors and protective tariffs against outsiders, apparently aids effective operation of this kind of organization.

Management is not alert to market opportunities. For example, no attempt is made to find out what consumers want as a guide to future production. Instead, goods are produced until they begin to clog the shelves of retail outlets. Then, on complaint from retail dealers, a new production line is undertaken and continued until the same process is repeated. Technical improvements come

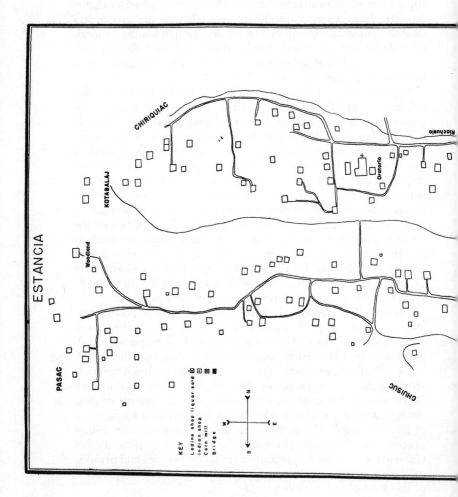

FIG. 5. Estancia.

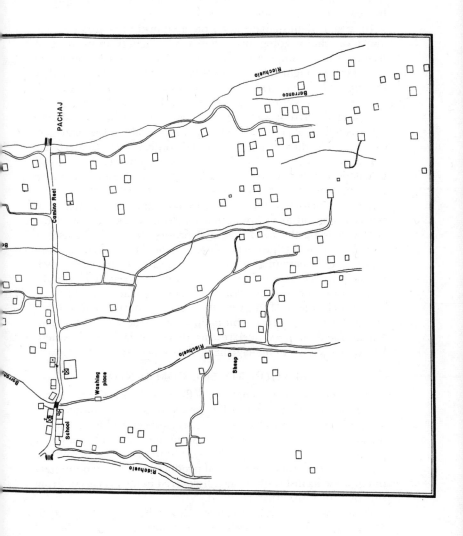

through obsolescence of some machines, which are then replaced by newer or more modern machines.

In actual plant management, the administrators are often unaware of what is going on in the factory. Figures on production trends, absenteeism, plant efficiency, and other indices from which management might calculate its policy, are in such a state that they are unusable. A government commission spent six weeks working over the firm's records to ascertain why the price of Cantel goods was pegged where it was, but even they were unable to make the records tell a coherent tale. The operating code of the managers in relation to the outside market and sources of raw materials is consequently one of "feel," only weakly buttressed by rational calculation based on records of production, sales, comparative costs, or other complex analyses.

Internal factory relations have been dominated by a mixture of paternalism and arbitrary authority. Prior to the advent of the union in 1945, the factory administrators concerned themselves with the personal adjustment of even the smallest internal disputes without differentiating levels of authority in handling such problems. Every request for, say, time off was taken to the administrator or to the owners' nephew for a personal hearing and decision; every hiring and firing went through the same procedure, often with a fatherly sermon on some malpractice of the man interviewed. Management of personnel reveals the same lack of consistent knowledge shown in management of production.

RELATION TO THE COMMUNITY

In the period since 1906, but chiefly since the 1930's the factory and community have gradually worked out an accommodation. Through mutual concessions, the basis has been laid for a smooth integration of the factory into the community, and of community personnel into the factory. The modifications which permit the factory to go about its business of production and the community to continue its institutions were discovered in the process of living side by side, rather than planned.

Factory work schedules take into account the traditional holidays of the community, as well as the traditional obligations of community members. Periods of fiesta, like the town fair and Easter Week, are not factory work periods. These long holidays are covered by Saturday afternoon overtime, not a usual period of factory operation. Neither production nor wages are reduced as a consequence of holidays. The four-hour period between shifts allows the factory worker with a small plot of land to attend to his agricultural duties without taking time off. It also permits women to do some of their household chores or to nurse small infants. If a man's turn comes up in one of the civil or religious offices the factory gives him time off, ranging from an afternoon to a two-year leave, without his suffering loss of job or tenure.

Not since the days of calling in troops in 1906 have the factory managers invoked extralocal sanctions in dealing with Canteleños. They found that in any problem relating to both community and factory it was easier to deal with the officials of the community. On their side, the officials learned that negotiation rather than threat was more useful in getting what they wanted. In short, the community did not try to run the factory, and the factory gave up trying to run the community. The discovery that points of friction could be resolved through meeting which resulted in small compromises by each party, is visible in the several community projects which factory and community have carried out together. In conjunction they built a bridge over the Samalá and cooperated in bringing in piped water. The factory paid for the new inlaid floor of the Pueblo church and financed the construction of the church in the factory area. It has donated to the upkeep of the roads, and has often lent technical aid such as loudspeakers, wiring, lighting, trucks, and personnel to village celebrations like the *fiesta titular*, the inauguration of civil and religious officials, and religious processions. On its side, the community allowed the factory's representative to bail out those jailed fiesta celebrants who were necessary to run machines. Cantel's unpaid police force often carries factory messages or relays public announcements the factory wants made.

The factory and community worked out these harmonious relations in response to their growing awareness of their mutual utility, in a situation in which the capital of the factory did not permit a change to an initially less hostile place, and the community did not intend to relinquish its highly prized autonomy and costumbre.

Another possible source of friction between factory and community, the presence of a large population of foreign workers, resolved itself. The early working force of mobile and uprooted Ladinos and Indians came to Cantel as a way station where new skills could be learned to move them upward in socioeconomic terms or outward to the larger centers of population. Movement to larger population centers coincides with the possibility of movement up the status hierarchy in Guatemala, so many of the early working force moved out of Cantel. The few who have remained engage in the same kinds of jobs as do the Canteleños, and their status and standard of living is therefore not greatly above the local level.

The factory's operation has not substantially changed Cantel's relations with nearby local communities. The factory's products are not in competition with the municipio's, so Cantel continues to

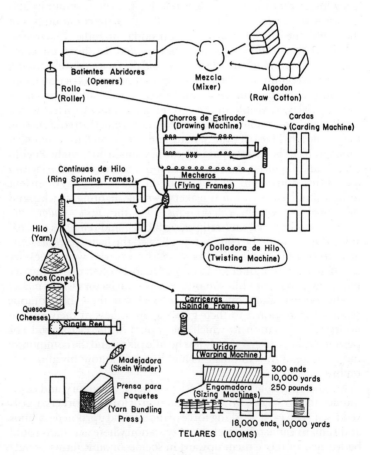

FIG. 6. Diagram of processes in the factory.

participate in subnational markets with the same kinds of goods. Neither has the factory turned Cantel into a center of commerce and movement, quickening its tempo of life and inviting new enterprise and new kinds of people. The one road that connects the Pueblo with Quezaltenango still serves the community and connects the factory with its sources of supply and points of distribution.

The Ladinos and foreign personnel (including non-native Indians), whose special skills are necessary to the factory, do not become members of the local community and hence do not intervene in its social life or concern themselves with it. They do not want to become part of the community, and could not even if they wanted to. They are isolated by differences in custom, language, social relations, and world view. The Cantel Indian makes a point of keeping them isolated. The Indian's elaborate show of deference to Ladinos and foreigners structures a social situation where intimacy is impossible and the exchange of cultural understanding is inhibited. When questioned by a Ladino, the Cantel Indian tries to find the answer he thinks the Ladinos want to hear, for this will terminate the interview as soon as possible with a contented, though possibly not informed, Ladino. Contact with local Ladinos is at a minimum, except for some intimacy between factory workers and Ladinos of the same status. Intercourse with Ladinos usually centers about some impersonal or economic situation in which the formal rules are clearly defined and create a transitory relationship. On their side, the Ladinos reinforce the ephemeral and impersonal qualities of interaction with Indians by their notions of ethnic superiority and the demands they make for respect and deference. At the same time, they expect Indians to be frank and open in responding to inquiry, on the assumption that Indians are "children with peaceful natures," without craft or artifice. This kind of interaction between Ladino and Indian in Cantel is a microexample of a mechanism for keeping their cultures apart which seems to be part of the adaptive mechanism of other Indian communities (Tax 1941; Gillin 1945).

If the cotton mill has not changed the relation of Cantel to other local communities, has not modified the channels of acculturation with the larger Guatemalan society nor affected the structure of ethnic relations, it has had the direct result of setting up new areas of activity with which Canteleño society and culture has had to cope. The direct tensions involved in operating the factory have been:

1. Modifying the settlement pattern in the provision of a secondary nuclear residence area.
2. Presenting an alternative economic opportunity entailing occupational roles requiring new behavior.
3. Employing Canteleños who traditionally would not be income producers.
4. Raising the net income of the municipio.
5. Aggregating workers under central direction in a production unit far greater in scale, in continuity of operation, and more complex in organization than any Cantel had ever exhibited.

In seeking the sources of change in the wake of the factory, and the responses of modification, innovation, conflict, or accommodation in the behavior of Canteleños, it is chiefly to these five factors that one must turn. These are the social pressures generated by the factory. The way people have interpreted them and have responded through their social groupings and cultural usages to these pressures and the problems they created make for the kind and degree of social and psychological change, or lack of it, that factory production has produced in the customs and personalities of the Cantelenses.

4

Factory Work: The Net Economic Advantage and the Occupational Role

MEETING A CUSTOMARY STANDARD OF LIVING

CANTELENSES have a definite notion of a style of life, seen chiefly in items of consumption and physical well being, which they call "adequate" or "customary" or "comfortable." The basis for the standard of living is usually expressed in terms of a family's wealth, rather than its income. Over and over it is said that 20 *cuerdas* of good, flat, well-watered land is what a family needs. What "a family needs" turns out to mean that a man, a woman, and three children can grow all the staples of corn, beans, and squash they consume, and still have enough surplus to sell in the market so that they may purchase the other things they will need.

ANNUAL INCOME ON 20 CUERDAS OF LAND

Item	Yield	Annual Price Range per Pound	Income in Lower Estimate	Income in Upper Estimate
Corn	4,000–5,000 lbs.	.04–.05½	Q184.00	Q233.00
Beans, black	200– 300 lbs.	.10	20.00	30.00
Beans, broad	200– 300 lbs.	.07	14.00	21.00
Squash	100– 160 units	.06–.10	8.00	10.00
Eggs	440	.05½–.06½	26.40	26.40
Wood	40 tarea	1.00	40.00	40.00
Other (fruit, guiscuiles, herbs)			25.00	
Total			317.40	360.40

Since a cuerda is equivalent to .108 acres, a family in Cantel must control 2.16 acres of land to live at the level which custom and aspiration call adequate. Translated into cash equivalents the produce from 2.16 acres is more than Q300, and apparently varies as widely as Q360 at the upper limit. On the basis of the harvests of 1953 and 1954, I checked yields per cuerda for farmers and selected two farmers of average skills and ordinary techno-logical aids for detailed figures on yields from their 20 cuerdas of land. Using a weighted average based on seasonal market price fluctuation, I converted the yields into income in the above table.

When Q300 annual income is placed against family budgets of those defined as comfortable in the community, the fact emerges that the Cantelenses calculate rather closely. A family of two adults and three children can easily meet its customarily defined standard of enough in quantity and quality and variety of food, religious fees, smoking and drinking, clothes that are not ragged, and other expenses.

From a land ownership census of Estancia, it appears that most Canteleños do not own 20 cuerdas of land; the average lies between 8 and 9, while the mode is between 0 and 4 cuerdas.

From the following table, it appears that 10 cuerdas of land is a breakpoint between factory and farm work. Factory work is preferred to farm work only if the farmer owns less than 10 cuerdas.

Many supplement their incomes by working as paid *mozos* (field hands) for other Cantelenses, by chopping trees and making planks from the forest in the communal land, by selling firewood, by keeping chickens and marketing eggs, or by selling the wool from their sheep. Some women embroider blouses on order or have other small income-producing specialties. Yet the majority of Cantel families do not have the income to live at the idealized standard. Older people told me that 20 cuerdas was "always" considered necessary for adequate living. I cannot say as to this, since both the standard and the level of living may have gone up since the coming of the factory. But it does seem that the normal functioning of the Cantel economic organization badly or in-adequately met a whole set of traditional wants and needs. They are still a poor people, and the spectre of degrading poverty is never far removed or often out of mind.

When it is asked, then, why Cantelenses came to the factory, the first answer is poverty. In the more than fifty interviews with persons employed in the factory, the reason given for coming to

OCCUPATION OF LANDOWNERS

Land Owned in Cuerdas	Factory Worker	Agricul- turalist	Specialist	Domestic	Total
None	12	45	14	1	72
1– 4	9	33	12	7	61
5– 9	2	10	1	4	17
10– 14	—	11	5	3	19
15– 19	1	11	4	—	16
20– 29	—	13	5	—	18
30– 39	—	7	2	—	9
40– 49	1	6	—	1	8
50– 59	—	5	—	—	5
60– 69	—	2	1	—	3
70– 79	—	2	—	—	2
80– 89	—	1	—	—	1
100–125	—	1	—	—	1
126–150	—	1	—	—	1
151–175	—	1	—	—	1
Total	25	149	44	16	234

the factory was couched in terms of economic need; "por necesidad," "ganar mi tamal," "hace la lucha," are the ways in which they say, "I was poor and the factory offered money." The land-ownership table shows that only two factory workers from Estancia own more than 10 cuerdas. And since factory wages are currently more than double the wages for *jornaleros* (day workers), the factory pay is a real and significant economic differential.

Money is important in this society. Everyone is engaged in buying and selling the necessities of life. Money is necessary to buy candles for daily religious worship at home, to pay for mass at life crises, to assume a religious office from which prestige flows, to buy the clothes that cover the body, to buy luxuries such as tobacco and liquor, to have a legal document drawn, and to pay for the utensils of the house or the implements of the field. In a thousand ways the wherewithal of life and the road to status and prestige is tied to money and to wealth. Thus the real economic differential of factory income is easily turned into acceptable items of cultural import through a recognized channel of pecuniary transactions common to all members of the community.

A real difference in income between factory and farm workers, coupled with the gap between ideal standard and the actual level of living, may be considered the propellent for seeking factory employment. Many of the factory workers were women and young men who, outside of the factory, would earn no income. For these classes of workers the factory represents a complete economic advantage, not merely a relative one in terms of alternate income possibilities.

The factory wage has certain other characteristics which make it appealing when contrasted with farming income. It has regularity and continuity. Agricultural return, both for hired hands and proprietors, has peaks and troughs corresponding to the harvesting, planting, and marketing cycle. Corn is planted in April and harvested in November. Wheat is planted in May and harvested in November and December. There is no local means of storing wheat, so it must be sold some time in January, after it has been threshed by the ancient method of horses walking in a circle. Corn is stored on the cob in roofed wooden bins. Most of the corn that finds its way to market is sold during the first three months after harvest. The maximum farm wages for those who must work on others' fields are received during the peak work periods of planting and harvesting. In April, May, June, October, November, and December all who seek paid farm work may find it. In September there is work for most in preparing fields, and in January there is work in clearing fields. Farm work is rare during the rest of the year. The tasks of weeding and of heaping earth at the base of each corn plant twice during the growing season do not employ the labor potential at anywhere near capacity. If a farm worker wants money in this off-season, he must engage in the supplemental occupations of barber, tailor, mason, brick-maker, or cut planks or sell fire-wood. The peak of income, often insufficient, is clustered for farmers and farm laborers in accord with the agricultural rhythm, while the need for cash is constant. However, the factory worker's income is more nearly matched to his need for money, and the regularity of income frequently obviates the need to borrow. Local interest rates are 20 to 25 percent per month, since Indians do not take advantage of bank loans and possibly would not be accepted if they applied.

The vicissitudes of agriculture are often great, given the Cantelense farming technology—a technology based on the machete, so useful in all agricultural tasks; a long iron rod for breaking ground; a short-handled *haz* or kind of scythe for cutting wheat; the knowledge of varieties of seeds and estimation of which seed grows best in what kind of land; and the imperfect and irregular fertilizing routine which utilizes only humus, animal wastes, and ashes. Yield from a cuerda varies from one hundred-weight of corn to three hundred-weight. Seasonal yields on the same land depend upon the weather, which is variable especially as to the strength and destructiveness of the *temporal*, the storm which caps the rainy season in late September or early October, just before the harvest. Sometimes, as in 1949, the crops of wheat and corn (and the beans and squash planted between the rows of maize and called collectively the *milpa*) are drastically cut by a bad storm. Though no years of famine are remembered in Cantel, there are lean and fat years.

The regularity and continuity of factory income are valued because Cantelenses like to be able to say that they are free of debt, independent and able to buy what they need when they need it. The factory worker gets what he calls the "centavo mas seguro"— the sure penny. The factory has worked without major stoppage since the end of the depression, so the sure penny comes in year after year as well as week after week.

In addition to the pull of wages, the factory offers social services. Housing is provided in 125 separate rent-free houses. These are not large nor do they have patios as do all other houses, however poor, but some are equipped with electricity, stronger than that of the Pueblo, the only other settlement which boasts electricity for a few private homes. The social importance of having or owning a house cannot be overestimated in Cantel, and this practice permits many to set up independent households who would otherwise be economically unable to.

The factory also maintains its own school, clinic, and doctor. The school has a six-hour day in contrast to the four-hour day of the national school; this longer school day is considered advantageous for the absorption of knowledge. The teachers in the factory school spend proportionately more time on reading, writing, and arithmetic than on practical arts. The school has better materials for teaching trades such as carpentry. Parents who have decided that knowledge of the national language, Spanish (usually a second language and learned in the school), and culture is as useful a tool or a means of personal or social mobility as are the trades, recognize the supposed advantage of the longer school day.

Medical facilities provided by the factory consist of a clinic where simple remedies are dispensed and medical advice and prescriptions are given. The doctor makes daily visits to the clinic at 5 P.M., and the nurse is always on hand. Important in the eyes of the Cantelenses is the nurse's prenatal service to the wives of factory workers and to female factory workers. Actual deliveries are still largely in the hands of midwives, and only 40 babies were delivered at the clinic in 1953. This society without birth control values the care and advice of doctor and nurse as safeguards to an easy delivery. Examination in the clinic is superficial and the remedies palliative, and the Cantelenses know they are not getting the kind of medical treatment they would receive if they were paying for it at a private physician's office. The doctor and clinic are a recourse for minor ills but this is still a service of some value, given the economic inability of the Cantelenses to take this sort of complaint to a doctor.

Until 1956, when the practice was discontinued, the factory owners sold each worker a supply of corn below market price. Each factory worker who so desired could buy 12 pounds of corn weekly at the fixed price of Q.03½ per pound. For 1954 the average price of corn was Q.04½ per pound, varying between Q.04 and Q.06. Since the traditional notion of security in Cantel is corn in the *troje*, food stored for the rest of the year rather than money in the bank, I thought this selling of corn provided a desirable dimension to factory work. But from observation in 1956, I could get no sense of deprivation from the workers when the corn ration was discussed. Apparently the economic meaning of the factory is chiefly the daily wage level and not the fringe benefits.

To some 30 to 40 percent of its workers, the factory loans up to two cuerdas of land. This loan of factory land may yield an increment to cash income as well as giving some of the landless a sense of ownership of soil, a strong value in this peasant community.

Factory work allows a man to become eligible for the Guatemalan system of social security, a kind of accident and health insurance rather than an old-age or retirement plan. A portion of each worker's wages and an equivalent contribution from the employer are paid to the national government, making the factory worker eligible for free ambulance service and hospital care for extended periods of time. There is no health service for the non-factory worker in Cantel.

Such are the economic dimensions of the factory's attractiveness: a clear and significant income differential, social and medical services, and the possibility of house or land provided by the factory. They have pull in a context of rural poverty and inadequate land resources.

ADAPTING TO A NEW OCCUPATIONAL ROLE

Between recruitment, which is accomplished by the factors enumerated, and commitment, which is personal involvement in the industrial work cycle, lies adjustment or adaptation to a new occupational role. The Canteleño in the factory finds himself working under conditions for which there are no homologies in his society or life experience. He often comes to the factory illiterate (for the past four or five years only "literates" have been hired), without previous experience with machinery of any kind—neither the gadgets of the housewife nor the motors and tools of Western men. The incoming worker is accustomed to small groups where work is carried out by men doing a variety of things rather than by division of labor which requires coordination and team work. The worker is used to setting his own rhythm of physical output, not adjusting to a machine tempo. He is accustomed to work without direction or supervision. He works with relatives or acquaintances, not strangers, choosing with whom he shall share effort. If he is tired or ill he need not go to his field, but the factory has a fixed hour for reporting and a fixed period of continual effort. In agricultural work, performances are judged by the farmer himself against a physical harvest; in the factory, output is measured by impersonal standards of so many inches of cloth, and there is no product which is the worker's own.

This discontinuity between the occupational roles of farm and factory workers sets the problem of the individual's accommodation to factory work.

LEARNING NEW WORK HABITS

New workers in the factory are trained by other Canteleños, in a manner similar to learning situations in the home and throughout childhood. A man or woman is hired as an assistant on some machine, say a weaving or spinning machine. For five or six weeks the newly hired worker performs menial tasks such as bringing material to the machine or taking finished goods off of it, but most of the time is spent in observing the operations of the person running the machine. I have spent hours watching a new employee learning a job. In one case a girl was learning to tend a loom. She would take her place at the side of the loom operator in the morning, bringing the cones of dyed cotton. Standing by the machine she watched the operator go through the motions of running the loom. She neither asked questions nor was given advice. When the machine snagged or stopped, she would look carefully to see what the operator did to get it back into motion. When a table cloth was woven, she removed it from the loom. This constituted her daily routine for nearly six weeks, and at the end of this time she announced that she was ready to run a loom. Her foreman told me that at no time during her learning and apprentice period had she touched a machine or practiced operating. When she said she was ready, the machine she had been observing for six weeks was turned over to her and she operated it, not quite as rapidly as the girl who had just left it, but with skill and assurance. What went on in the "training" period? The apprentice was applying the way of learning she had been taught in Cantel. She observes and internally rehearses the set of operations until she feels able to perform. She will not try her hand until she feels competent, for to fumble and make mistakes is a cause for *vergüenza*—public shame. She does not ask questions because that would annoy the person teaching her, and they might also think she is stupid. After sufficient observation the apprentice arrives at the point where she feels that she can carry on the necessary physical operations. I have observed this method of learning among the home weavers with their young apprentices, among the young boys who learn to drive cars, and even in the case of a man who was learning to sing but never sang a note until after a five or six hour session of just listening. In this way the recruit is inducted into his new job and its new skills easily and according to customary training patterns.

This method of learning no doubt has severe limitations and may not function when the learning is symbolic or of purely mental operations, but it works in teaching the simple tasks of running cotton textile machines. Management reports six weeks as about the upper limit of anyone learning to run a loom or a spinning machine. I am told that operating the more complex jacquard requires more learning time, and the factory looks for the *listos*, the bright ones, among its working forces to train as operators. But for other operations the illiterate farmer or housewife, a stranger to machinery, is converted into a reasonably proficient factory hand in six weeks.

The learning process is slightly modified when a Cantelense learns to be a caporal, machine shop worker, or assistant in the electrical shop. Here the technical staff gives verbal instruction and explains the principles and operations of the machine or instrument. The technical staff complains that Cantelenses do not practice and often make costly mistakes when they think they can operate one of the more complex machines. In the more skilled jobs, the complaint is that Cantelenses are often "indifferent and unenthusiastic" when they learn. This complaint of the foreign technical staff is a recognition of the Cantelense desire to appear calm and dignified, even when a neophyte may be eager to learn new skills.

Factory training, where results are rapidly achieved, contrasts with the training situation in the school. Teachers say it is difficult to get performance, and Cantelenses say that too much school work or thinking makes the head *caliente*, hot, and leads to minor illness.

FACTORY VS. FARM WORK

If entry into the factory is made easy, working in it is not much more difficult. Getting to work each morning at a fixed hour is little trouble for the Canteleño. The normal rising hour is between 4 A.M. and 5 A.M., and this allows the worker to report at 6 A.M. without modification in habit. There was a time when late reporting was chronic. The factory manager instituted a program of locking the factory doors at two minutes after the morning whistle, so that those who were late lost a day's pay, rather than an hour or two. Pay loss, coupled with the shame of being locked out and having to go home, seemed sufficient to end late reporting. Close punctuality, not germane to the work routine outside of the mill, apparently is not so much of a personal strain as is the deprivation of a day's wages.

Factory work does not entail a different division of the day from that of other occupations in Cantel. Meals are taken at the same time, and the leisure pattern is not violated. A farmer works every day except Sunday, certain feast days, Easter Week, and the titular fair. So does the factory worker, except that he works on several

feast days which the farmer is likely to observe. After a day's work
the pattern is to go to sleep. Visiting and playing during the week
are virtually absent and morally frowned upon. None of my factory
informants complained about the loss of feast days, which is more
than offset by the free Saturday afternoon of the factory schedule.

The only possibly serious break in the daily routine might have
come for nursing mothers, but the factory allowed them an extra
half-hour in the morning and afternoon to feed infants brought
in by servant girls or relatives. The four hours off during the day,
on whatever shift is worked, permits the worker to attend to
necessary household tasks. Working in the factory therefore does
not reorient the time axes of social participation or of customary
allocation of time outside of the work cycle.

Once inside the factory, the day's work of constant effort is under
way. Almost without exception, the Cantelenses regard factory
work as *mas suave*, easier or lighter than labor in the field, where
they must work under the hot sun, exposed to the frequent high
winds and often to the chill rain. The factory, say the workers, is
dry, not too hot or cold, and there is no wind. After the customary
eight-hour day of wielding the heavy hoe or picking corn or carrying hundredweights of grain on the back with a tump-line, the field
hand is tired. Agricultural work is heavy and hard, and in seasons of
breaking ground for planting and in harvesting and carrying, the
farmer is so tired at the end of a day's work that he commonly says
"my back aches." Hard work, sweat on the brow, and calluses on
the hand are valued in Cantel culture, and a man grows up expect-
ing to work hard and end each day spent and tired. A Cantelense
will say it is wicked to be idle; it is immoral to earn without labor;
it is pernicious to complain because one must toil to eat. Rather,
one should "da gracias a Díos" for strength and health to work,
even in the factory.

HOUSEWIFE VS. CAREER GIRL

The housewife's task load as compared to the female factory
worker's is such that neither gets much of an edge in terms of
physical expenditure. The housewife rises at 4:30 or 5 A.M. and
hauls the morning water from the nearest *pila* in a jug balanced on
her head. She prepares the morning meal, grinding the *nixtamal*
(corn grains cooked with lime water) three times if she uses the
electric mill and five times if she does not. She grinds in a kneeling
position, pushing a stone rolling pin against a stone table set on

three short legs in a swift back and forth motion. She cooks in a smoke-filled kitchen on a wood fire circled by the three-stone *tenemaste* which supports the earthen and metal pots, jugs, and other utensils. She watches constantly, occasionally stirring the liquids or turning the *tortilla* toasting on the pottery griddle. More often than not, she has a young child strapped to her back while doing her chores. All through the day she repeats these acts to prepare the meals. She also washes dishes and serves her husband and older male children at mealtimes. She washes clothing by carrying a heavy load down to the river or to a communal washing place, and carrying the wet clothes on her head back to her patio for drying. She mends clothing, buys and sells in the market place, and arranges the patio and cleans the house. The typical housewife is always busy and always pressed for time. Cantel women walk rapidly in the streets, and loitering is frowned upon. An idle woman is not *cumplido*—not fulfilling her housewifely duties in a competent manner. Cantel women are not given to complaint about the burdens of housework and domestic life, but they like it to be known that this is a full-time task—that one does not have time to stop and gossip in the streets, nor to visit, nor to sit idle. The physical demands of housework, not alleviated as they might be in a gadget-prone North American home, at least match factory work if they do not surpass it. Housewives do not relinquish all household duties when they come to the factory, but as a rule they take on an unmarried girl as a *criada* (servant of all work), full-time if the factory woman has small children and for occasional tasks if not. They may shift some of the domestic work to other women if they live in a multifamily household. Their income compensates for such delegation of housework.

Since every woman is expected to be first of all a housewife, the career woman has not developed among the Indians. Few women with primary households under their exclusive care work in the factory. Their husbands object on the grounds of sexual suspicion, and most women share the belief that the children of women who work in the factory die with greater frequency than the offspring of women who give their full time to the home.

TEMPO AND ROUTINE OF WORK

The tempo of the machines requires constant attention and care, but such application does not appear to be a major factor in the adjustment to industrial work. The Cantelense will not take more machines to tend nor run one faster than he comfortably can, despite the incentive of piece work. Compared to North American mill hands, the factory managers report that the Cantel worker is slower and runs fewer machines. Whether this is due to the worker or to the age of the machine and its disposition in relaton to the task, I do not know. But the pace of the machines does not appear man-killing, and the Canteleños say it is not. The unaccustomed posture of standing all day or using the same set of muscles all day is not considered much of a strain. The minor changes in body work rhythm and in constant application required by the machine are taken to easily by the Cantelenses, and I could not elicit one complaint about factory work on that score. From watching Cantelenses run machines, it appears that changes in motor habits and working strains do not require much psychological reorientation or occasion physiological crises. For the majority the shift in work pattern is not a jolt, but at most only a little ripple which in a year or so is not even easily recalled, and questioning about the problem usually brings blank stares or long pauses while memory is ransacked for "difficulties" in adapting body tempo to machine tempo. Those who did not adjust to the tempo have left the factory, and of the ones to whom I have talked, none who are now engaged in economic activity left because of the difficulty or strangeness of the work. Only one man, whose bare feet on the wet concrete floor of the dyeing room bothered him, complained to me that he found factory work more unpleasant than farm work.

SUPERVISION AND DISCIPLINE

Working in coordination or under orders does not appear to make factory work less desirable. Work at the machines is co-ordinated by a caporal in charge of a line of machines. He is a Cantelense. He and the worker he directs understand each other. The caporal never raises his voice when giving directions, and rarely tells a man what to do. Only occasionally does he call out "apúrate," or hurry up, when someone slows down at his machine. If the worker is on piece work, he is more likely to call out to the caporal to adjust the machine if it is stalled or slowed. The caporal's authority is limited by his sense of how it should be exercised; that is, he does not order but rather suggests what is to be done. Workers seldom complain that they have been mistreated or that a caporal is unreasonable in his demands.

Before the organization of the union, the supervision and

discipline routine was less to the taste and custom of Cantel. The foreign engineer, not bound by conventional understandings as to the proper exercise of authority, was wont to circulate about the room and slap laggards across the head. The factory owners on their periodic visits did the same. Physical force and abusive language were used by the factory owner and the technical staff to get things done in the way they wanted them done. The workers always objected to this treatment, since being publicly reprimanded is scandalous and shameful, and being struck as a means of correction puts one in the category of a child. I cannot judge how great a factor this discipline was in labor turnover prior to the union; it was not given as a reason in any of the cases of which I have record. However, the union frowned on physical punishment of any sort. The British engineer struck a worker who had ruined an expensive machine, and the union brought a complaint against him; he was asked to make a public apology to the worker in the presence of the manager. This affirmed the principle, operative since the late 1940's, that discipline was the job of the caporal. Caporales could use any means except insult and corporal punishment.

There is little status difference and no sentimental differential between the caporal and the worker in his line. Both are workers, distinct from the clerical staff and the managerial interests. In exercising his authority, which stems from the imperatives of keeping the machines operating and coordinating work so that the flow of materials does not occasion lags between operations, the caporal takes his orders from the technical staff and passes them on to the line worker according to the impersonal needs of the job. But the way in which he gives orders is in terms of Cantel notions about how men are to be treated when they work for each other. The caporal is a worker who gets slightly more pay; he is not of, and not necessarily for, the management. Outside the factory walls the foreman's prestige is no greater than that of mill hand. Inside the mill, the caporal does not flaunt his authority nor give many or unnecessary instructions and commands, and neither his dress nor his language mark him off from the machine hand.

Strict observance of the cultural definitions of authority and its legitimate exercise by the caporal gives supervision and discipline the same tone as the organization of simpler work groups in the agricultural tasks. The virtual status coincidence of caporal and line worker insulates the management from the workers, and keeps the owners in the dark as to why one set of machines turns out only so much when they think it should be producing more. The pace on a line of machines is set by the more experienced workers, and the others, including the caporal, take it as the given pace.

If the relationship between caporal and worker serves to isolate management from worker, it paradoxically encourages the paternalistic relationship between worker and employer, so common in Latin enterprises. Since the caporal is not an intermediary, the worker expresses his grievances directly to the patrón—the owner or white-collar employee. Prior to unionization, and even afterward, the smallest grievances were carried directly to the patrón. In our conception of him as policy maker or entrepreneur he would never concern himself with settlement of such picayune affairs, but he personally collected information and handled the problem in a face-to-face way. This mode of dealing with complaint and allegation is paralleled in community life by the alcalde's personal and prompt dispatch of civil grievances.

THE ROLE OF THE UNION

The *sindicato*, or labor union, is important in making the factory attractive to Canteleños. The emergence of the workers' organization is recounted in a later section. The union welded the worker to his job through these obvious ways: it gave him a greater economic return; it allowed the swift and direct airing of grievances; it gave some control over the job and conditions of work; it involved the worker in a set of social relations based on voluntary membership; it taught him some elementary lessons of pressure group tactics and effective organization; it gave the workers closer ties to the nation through the network of a national labor movement.

The union was community-oriented and played a part in many community projects, buttressing the integration of workers into their community. I emphasize the union's ability to aid in the individual's commitments to the factory, not only on the grounds of the wage and work gains but because this estimate of the union's role was made plain to me in late 1954. When the union went into a temporary period of inaction following the overthrow of the Arbenz government (all social groupings connected in any way with the national government had a similar period of suspension until the character of the Armas regime was crystallized), 32 men quit their jobs within a week. This was the largest turnover in the decade and it arose from the real possibility, which did not materialize, that the union was to be totally and permanently abolished.

The net economic advantage of factory work and the character of the occupational role account for the recruitment of the factory labor force, and during the last decade for its firm commitment to industrial wage work as a way of making a living. I have attempted elsewhere (Nash 1956) to generalize on the emergence of a committed labor force on the basis of Cantel's successful experience.

If the fact of an alternative economic role in the factory did not necessitate behavioral changes which conflicted with customary work patterns, nor result by itself in modifying other modes of behavior, then it is to the other factors, enumerated earlier as tensions set up by the factory, that we must turn to account for the kind of social and cultural change that took place in Cantel.

5

The Social and Cultural Life : Comparison of Factory and Farm Work

WHAT I have called tensions introduced by the factory are produced for individuals by new income, more and continual contact with nonkinsmen in the work situation, and a scheduling of their energy, and leisure in terms of factory instead of farm. With these shifts of time, energy, and resources, individuals have opportunities of combining elements so that new patterns of social relations, new goals and new activities may emerge. On the face of it, the factory worker has a range of alternatives, areas of choice not immediately present to those engaged in traditional occupations. We may borrow an epigram from Firth and say that "change is the implication of choice." How far have factory workers wanted or been able to reorganize the pattern of their lives? Have they become different in their style of life, religious sentiment, familial routines, consumption habits, wants and needs, or world view from those not in the factory?

To answer this query I have analytically compared the two occupational segments, factory versus agriculture. Since most factory workers are recruited from the farming segment, and the return to agricultural work is infrequent, point-by-point comparison emphasizes the bases on which choices are (or are not) made to do new or different things. I stress the mechanisms of social control which have inhibited the making or implementing of decisions capable of radically differentiating the factory from the agricultural segment.

LEVEL OF LIVING

The comparison of factory-employed persons with agriculturalists as to their level of living revolves on the axes of choice open to the factory wage worker. More income provides the basis for implementing a larger range of desires and for modifying the style of life from the traditional basis. The material aspects of the factory

44

worker's life are an index to his subscription to Cantel's cultural budget of preferences, on the one side, or the organization of expenditure to express a culturally alternative set, on the other.

Most factory workers live in the Pueblo or the factory settlement, with a few scattered among the rural cantones. The houses which factory workers either buy or build for themselves (this excludes the factory housing which shelters just over 10 percent of the factory employees) are within the range of house types familiar to all Cantelenses. A worker's home cannot be distinguished on architectural grounds alone from the run of Cantel dwelling places. The most frequently encountered houses in Cantel are one-story structures of adobe brick, topped by a tile roof pitched at a 45 degree angle. The rooms may lie in a row opening upon a patio, an open space enclosed by an adobe wall of four to eight

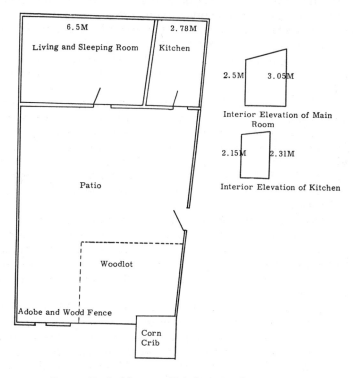

FIG. 7. Typical house of inhabitants of the Pueblo.

feet in height, or they may form an "L" with two openings on the patio. Figure 7 gives the physical layout of the typical Pueblo house. Deviations from this type are of two kinds in the Pueblo: two-story houses, with the second story used only for storage, and the longer five-room "hallway" pattern which often houses multiple families. Two-story houses, of which there are but three, are all on the plaza and belong to the richest families in Cantel.

The main dwelling units of these houses consist of one or two rooms; each room has an entrance but there are no connecting doors. The door into the patio is kept open in the daytime to admit light and air. Rarely does a house have glazed windows. The bare earthen floors are covered with pine needles only for festivities. In the main room are usually a few benches or chairs, a table holding the household image surrounded by flower-filled vases and candles and incense plates, and one or more plain wooden beds. If there is another room, beds, *cofres*, and miscellaneous articles are kept there. Only the richest homes have a living room without beds. On the board beds is either a straw-stuffed mattress or simply a straw *petate*; blankets are the Momostenango wool or a cheaper flannel from Mexico, which is now becoming more popular.

The kitchen is usually a separate structure, but may be attached to the living rooms. It contains a profusion of pottery jugs, *comales, jarros*, grinding stones of various sizes, wooden ladles and spoons, net bags, woven straw bags, water containers, pitchers, and Mexican enamelware plates and cups. The utensils are stacked on wooden shelves or hung from nails. On the floor opposite the entrance is the three-stone hearth, sometimes hedged by a circle of flat stones.

Figure 8 gives the physical layout of a house in Estancia. It is typical of the rural dwelling, where thatched houses are most common and where the mass adobe house is sometimes found. Figure 9 is a sketch of the factory provided house. It varies from the Cantel range in not having a patio and is more restricted in room space.

The size of a house, its state of repair, whether or not its adobe walls are covered with tinted whitewash, depend in part on wealth. But factory workers' houses do not vary in any consistent way from other houses. The factory workers' income advantage is not spent on the house beautiful, and even their kitchens show the same slapdash arrangement of utensils, the three-stone hearth, the

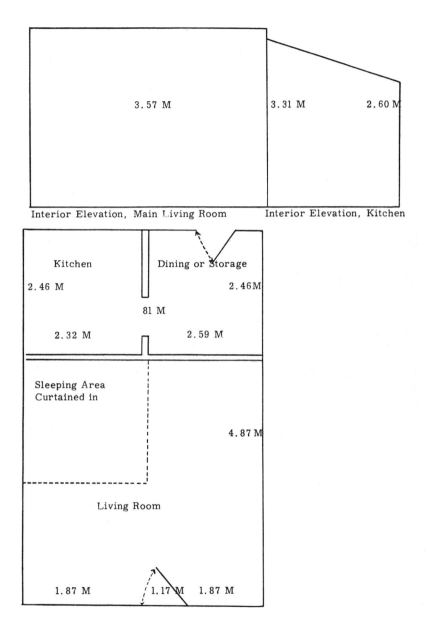

Interior Elevation, Main Living Room   Interior Elevation, Kitchen

FIG. 9. Diagram of a typical factory-owned house let to factory workers.

The table on p. 51 compares two factory families, representing the average budgets of that segment; one farm family, close to the adequate standard set by farmers, and a representative Ladino family. It is evident that workers spend a greater part of their food budget on meat, vegetables, and bread, and that their corn consumption decreases. Workers' budgets show that they are well within the Cantel Indian pattern of consumption, when compared to the Ladino family. All of the items in factory diets are consumed at some time during the year by farmers, but the factory family tends to use them continually and in greater quantity than do farm families.

CLOTHING

On an ordinary working day it is difficult to distinguish factory and farm individuals by dress or costume. A careful count would show that factory workers are more often shod than are nonfactory; that factory women wear sandals with rubber soles more frequently than do farmers' wives; and that there are more felt than straw hats among factory workers. But the overlap is great and the factory group does not stand out. On fiesta days, however, the economic advantage of factory work is apparent in the relative luxury of apparel. During Easter Week and the fair in honor of the patron saint, it is customary to *echar el cofre encima*, that is to don one's best clothes which have been stored in wooden boxes and set apart for just such occasions. Factory workers are uniformly better dressed than farmers and their families. Women appear in skirts which are bright and almost new, in the most expensive kind of *huipiles* with elaborate silk and cotton embroidery, with ribbons of shiny new rayon in their hair, with a shawl of the most costly tie-and-dye material, with silver necklaces and earrings, and almost invariably with footwear. Farm women may approach this holiday splendor, but given the low level of income among the peasantry as a whole, many appear in clean but obviously worn clothing. Some appear with plain cotton blouses and faded skirts, barefoot, and with old shawls bleached by innumerable washings.

Men exhibit the same kind of differences in newness and finery, but in addition many factory men have taken on modern Western attire. The whole Quezaltenango valley shows a trend in this direction, but Cantel factory men appear in the forefront of the movement to shift male attire from the Indian version to Ladino style. If a male wears a jacket longer than the Indian

WEEKLY FOOD CONSUMPTION (QUANTITY AND VALUE) OF 4 CANTEL FAMILIES

| | Indians | | | | | | Ladino Family | |
	Factory Family 1		Factory Family 2		Farm Family			
Corn, lbs.	40	$1.52	37½	$1.44	50	$2.22	28	$ .82
Lime, lbs.	1	.03	1	.03	1	.03	1	.03
Black beans, lbs.	4	.40	4	.40	3	.36	2	.20
White beans, lbs.	—	—	—	—	—	—	—	—
Lima beans, lbs.	4	.28	3	.21	—	—	2	.17
Chile, oz.	—	—	2	.06	8	.16	—	—
Green chile, oz.	4	.24	—	—	—	—	—	—
Salt, lbs.	1	.04	1	.04	1	.04	1	.04
Coffee, lbs.	1	.50	½	.20	1	.40	1	.40
Low refined sugar, lbs.	4	.40	3	.30	4	.52	—	—
White sugar, lbs.	2	.16	2	.19	2	.16	7	.56
Chocolate	—	—	1	.32	—	—	—	—
Bread (rolls)	25	.50	25	.50	13	.26	35	.70
Rice, lbs.	2	.22	1	.12	—	—	2	.22
Noodles, lbs.	½	.12	½	.13	—	—	1	.24
Oatmeal, lbs.	—	—	—	—	—	—	2	.30
Macaroni, lbs.	—	—	—	—	—	—	1	.24
Pepper, oz.	—	—	¼	.05	1/10	.02	—	—
Cloves, oz.	—	—		.01	—	.02	—	—
Cinnamon	—	—	—	—	—	.03	—	—
Eggs, doz.	½	.36	⅓	.24	⅙	.12	2½	1.80
Milk, liter	1.8	.21	3½	.42	—	—	1½	.18
Cheese, lbs.	—	—	1	.12	—	—	—	—
Beef with bone, lbs.	4	.88	4	.22	1½	.33	3	.66
Beef without bone, oz.	—	—	10	.22	—	—	—	—
Tongue, lbs.	—	—	—	—	—	—	2	.68
Pork with bone, lbs.	—	—	1½	.32	—	—	—	—
Pork blood sausage, oz.	—	—	4	.15	—	—	—	—
Lard Cracklings, oz.	—	—	—	—	—	—	4	.12
Lard, lbs.	1	.40	½	.20	½	.20	2	.80
Tomatoes, lbs.	2	.16	1	.12	2	.20	6	.24
Potatoes, lbs.	6	.36	3	.15	—	—	6	.33
Onions	6	.05	12	.06	12	.10	24	.20
Garlic, bunch	1	.02	—	—	—	—	—	—
Cabbage, head	2	.16	1	.05	1	.10	1	.04
Carrots, bunch	2	.08	1	.04	—	—	2	.12
Radishes	—	—	2	.03	—	—	1	.04
Cauliflower, head	2	.16	1	.06	—	—	—	—
Turnips, bunch	2	.10	—	—	—	—	2	.06
Green beans	—	—	—	—	—	—	—	—
Beets	6	.04	—	—	—	—	12	.12
Peas, lbs.	3	.18	—	—	—	—	2	.10
Lettuce, head	—	—	—	—	—	—	1	.04
Chiltepe, oz.	—	—	2	.04	—	—	—	—
Oranges	—	—	—	—	—	—	4	.04
Limes, lb.	1	.03	1	.03	1	.03	1	.03
Sapodillas	—	—	—	—	—	—		.05
Bananas	12	.04	—	—	10	.05	8	.16
Plantains, doz.	1	.28	—	—	—	—	—	—
Comiels	—	—	—	—	—	.02	—	—
Sweets	—	—	—	—	—	—	—	.05

standard of waist length, if it is of worsted wool rather than the cotton of Cantel or the hand-woven wool of Momostenango or San Francisco El Alto, or should the jacket and trousers form a suit with some kind of pattern, then the man is a local Ladino or a factory worker. A tie, or socks with shoes, also mark a local Ladino or an Indian factory worker, not farmers. Not all factory workers have shifted to the Ladino model but all of the shifts are within the factory groups, with the exception of two farm families high on the wealth scale, and one highly literate and acculturated Indian. The dress of factory females has remained Indian, becoming richer and more luxurious but not departing from traditional form or content.

The departure in dress is based only partly on income advantage. It represents greater access to Ladino models, along with the notion of clothing as display. The occupational role is symbolically visible only in times of celebration.

THE FAMILY

The Cantel nuclear family is composed of a man, his wife, and their unmarried offspring, living together in their own household. This nuclear family traces descent through both the mother's and father's lines and is thus tied to a wide network of bilateral kin. The nuclear family is the unit of consumption, production, ritual performance, child rearing, and religious activity. It is the family which has a social status in the community, and it is the family, rather than individuals, which takes turns in the discharge of civil and religious offices. Still, this is not a kinship society, and other aspects of the social structure, as will be seen later, are equally important in the daily round of activity. I refer to the nuclear family in a network of bilateral kindred as the familial atom of the social structure because it is the most frequent form of family organization, and it is the ideal pattern toward which Cantelenses strive. The dynamics of family life are understandable only if the preferred form of family organization, the nuclear, is seen as the one pattern which does not arouse tensions or occasion frustrations.

Cantel household composition is actually of three kinds: nuclear, paternal joint, and compound family. The variation in family composition is part of the social structure. Any social structure contains patterns of organization which deviate from the norms, and which represent the structure's capacity to tolerate variability. The presence of the three kinds of families in Cantel is apparently a long-standing fact. From the presence of old multiple-family houses, from the reports of old informants, and from old records, it appears that familial variety has been the rule. In 1954, 78.8 percent of the 860 families for which I have complete census data were nuclear; the remaining 21.2 percent were some form of joint or compound household. The relative frequency of household type among factory and nonfactory segments is virtually identical. This similar incidence indicates that the gross sociological features of Cantel family organization have been little modified by the presence of the factory.

A look at the dynamics of family formation will make clear why factory work has not greatly shifted the incidence of kinds of families, and why the social structure and its variation therefore continues to be perpetuated. When a man marries in Cantel, it is customary for him to take up residence with his father for a short period. It is his hope that his father will give him some land or capital so that he can set up his own household. The paternal joint family is viewed as inherently unstable, and the married son will move as soon as there is an economic base to do so. This base consists of a house and house site and, traditionally, land capable of supporting the household. The social importance of one's own household cannot be overestimated; in fact, it is being head of one's own household that makes a man an adult member of the community.

Paternal joint families or other compound families, where they are stable, are compromise family situations which deny one of the nuclear families its full social position. The compromises are based on a man's inability to implement the cultural norm, and this inability is of two kinds. Either he is so poor (or his parents are so poor) that an independent household is not feasible; nor his father is so rich that he can hold on to one son's family by the promise of a larger inheritance.

Factory workers have been able to shorten the period of patrilocal residence and to move into separate households earlier than farm equivalents. But factory income does not permit the permanent establishment of joint families, nor provide any social basis for their formation. At the same time that factory families can form separate households on the basis of factory income, they permit farm families to compete for more land; therefore, farm families also tend to reduce the period of patrilocal residence. The net effect of the factory has been to keep viable the cultural norm of separate nuclear families. But because factory workers often take economic responsibility for aged parents, they too have compound families, thus reversing the usual dependency pattern.

The one apparent modification is the consistent trend toward the shortening of patrilocal residence. According to older informants, this has been the case for some time. It is entirely possible that patrilocal residence may eventually cease (as service to wife's family has virtually ceased) in the wake of the economic possibility of formation of a separate family household without great aid from the parents.

The gross similarity in the composition of factory and farm families is thus maintained by varying mechanisms. The virtually identical frequencies of family form mask these minor variations in economic and residence aspects of the factory family.

Comparison of a Factory Worker's and a Farmer's Family

The economic and residence dimensions of family formation only partly explain the persistence of family structure. The intimate aspects of domestic life, the sets of attitudes between relatives, and the common tasks and rewards of kinsmen play as large a role. I take here for comparison the family of a factory worker, Juan Q., and the family of an independent farmer, Reginio M. These men are nearly the same age, as are their wives. They have about the same annual income, approximately Q370, and the same number of children. (This annual income is what the Cantelenses call "adequate" and is above the prevailing level of living. It is reasonable to assume that these families implement with their higher incomes the culturally desirable way of life.) They are both native Canteleños, clearly Indian. I have selected them as a basis for discussion because they vary chiefly in the single dimension of occupation, and I have been intimately acquainted with both households for long periods. The contrast between them bares the mechanism of social control in domestic life and serves as a base line against which to project the forms of family variation in Cantel.

Both families live in their own dwelling unit. The factory worker lives in the town center, about three blocks off the main plaza, and the farmer lives in the rural canton of Pachaj. When they say *familia*, both men mean their nuclear family. In concept and practice the nuclear family is the only kin group, and it is embedded in kinship ties collectively called the *wačla.l*—the familiars.

Relationship of the Nuclear Family to the Extended Kindred

The nuclear families of the two men are strikingly alike in their relations with their respective kindreds. For both, meaningful relationships within the wide-ranging, loosely defined wačla.l depend upon personal cultivation. The kindred is a set of possible relationships which may never turn out to be perduring social relationships. The kindred, never complete, assembles only at life crises—births, weddings, and funerals. Reginio maintains close ties with his sister, brother, an uncle, and his paternal cousins. With the exception of his late father, his brother and sister are the most important to him. They live near him, and they are the only people he feels free to visit without a pretext. But the duties they owe him, and which he owes them, are not fixed. He does not expect to receive economic aid from them, or help in cultivating his fields. His ties to them are sentimental and emotional, and mean no more than an easy situation in which he can be a whole person.

Juan's wačla.l similarly consists of vague and unspecified ties to bilateral kinsmen. His kindred assembled only at the wedding of one and at the funeral of another of its members, and once at Christmas. It has no economic unity. Juan may call on members of his kindred for aid in time of illness, or perhaps for consultation about land transfer, but when he needs money he goes to a local money lender. His wife draws on members of her kindred for aid in fiesta cooking or to help with a sick child, but she is as likely to draw on her husband's kin as on her own. The kinship terminology employed by Juan and Reginio reflects the nature of the kindred (Figure 10). Juan's memory goes back only two generations. He can name his father's and mother's brothers and sisters, but in the grandparental generation he knows only his grandfather and grandmother. There are no kinship terms in his vocabulary for the brothers and sisters of his grandparents. Of this generation only the grandparents, who may give moral counsel, are socially important. His parents, as well as his siblings, also give counsel and help instruct his children, but they have no disciplinary powers over either Juan or the children. He would take it badly if his brothers or sisters or parents physically chastised his children. For Juan and Reginio, as well as for their wives, the most important

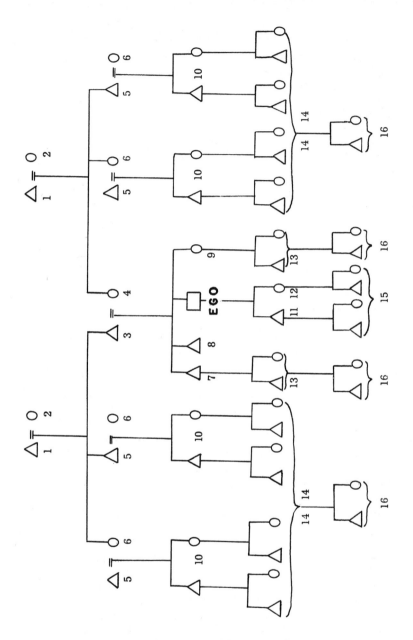

Fɪɢ. 10. Consanguineal kin terminology.

social bonds outside of the nuclear family are the sibling bonds and the respect relationship to parents. The women of these two families maintain closer ties to their mothers than do the men, and sisters tend to be more intimate and to share more activities than do brothers.

The respective kindreds should be viewed as sets of respect relationships, with opportunities to ask things of kinsmen one would not ask of a stranger. But whether or not one seeks out a kinsman depends as much upon mutual attractions and personal adjustments as it does upon the kinship tie. In such a kinship system, it is not strange that factory work has not occasioned expansion, contraction, or more intense cultivation of kin ties.

Relationships within the Nuclear Family

In relationships internal to the families of which Reginio and Juan are chief earners and heads, the same pattern of dominance and relative position is seen. The male head is dominant, the age and sex principles operate as between siblings, and should either Juan or Reginio visit the other, he would find the prevailing set of relationships within the other's household completely understandable and worthy of approval.

In his family Juan is the center of authority. He is also the center of attention and solicitude. His *wušokil* (wife) addresses him by name in private, but this is not to be taken as an understanding of equality. She is subordinate to his will, and his needs come first. The children in the family are in respect and subordination relations with both Juan and Roberta, but Juan is the clear figure of power and of final say. Juan's position of authority is visible in most of the social interaction in the household. At mealtime he is served first; he sits with his only son, the youngest child, at the table while his wife squats on the floor taking her food only after they have been served. When he leaves the house, his wife does not question where he goes or when he will return; it is sufficient for him to say he has an errand to perform. Between husband and wife is a division of labor along sex lines, with the children having lesser roles, according to their age. Juan is the breadwinner in the factory. He is also responsible for minor repairs of the house and for buying all the major items of furnishing. Roberta cleans, cooks, markets, launders, and takes charge of the children, with some assistance from the older daughter. She hauls water from the pila, clears the patio, grinds the corn, serves the meals, and keeps

CONSANGUINEAL KINSHIP TERMINOLOGY*

No.	English	Spanish	Quiché	
			Male Ego	Female Ego
1	My grandfather	mi abuelo	numa.m	numa.m
2	my grandmother	mi abuela	watit	watit
3	my father	mi papa	nuta.t	nuta.t
4	my mother	mi mama	nunan	nunan
5	my uncle	mi tio	nuti.ya	nuti.ya
6	my aunt	mi tia	nuti.ya	nuti.ya
7	my older brother	mi hermano mayor	wuƚ	nučaⱪ
8	my younger brother	mi hermano menor	nučaⱪ	nučaⱪ
9	my sister	mi hermana	wanaƀ	wanaƀ
10	my first cousin	mi primo/a hermano/a	pri.m wačla.l	pri.m wačla.l
11	my son	mi hijo	nukuxe.l	wa.l
12	my daughter	mi hija	numiya.l	wa.l
13	my nephew (niece)	mi sobrino/a	sobri.n	sobri.n
14	my cousin	mi primo/a	pri.m	pri.m
15	my grandson (daughter)	mi nieto/a	ʔuwinuma.m	ʔuwinuma.m
16	my relative	mi pariente	wačla.l	wačla.l

*Quiché terms are not exact semantic equivalents of Spanish or English terms.

the house. Juan punishes the children, usually at her behest.
There is never an open display of affection between husband and wife. Love terms, nicknames, casual gestures of endearment are absent in daily life. The husband's affection is expressed by carrying out the duties of the role and by not beating his wife too frequently or without due cause. The woman shows attachment by doing her household duties, by fidelity to her husband, by helping him home when he is drunk, and by not walking much alone in the streets. The children are expected to show great deference to both parents. They never use first names, but always use the formal *tat* for father and *nan* for mother. The parents may use endearing terms like *mamacita* or *papacito*, for a female or male child respectively. The children, if small, as in Juan's house, never interrupt when the adults are talking and always wait to be spoken to before speaking. The younger one may upset this ideal pattern by crying, but when he is old enough to understand he may take his place as

a quiet member of the family. The mother demonstrates more affection toward the children than does the father. He is considered to have exhibited his concern for the children by providing them with food, clothing, shelter, and education, and medicine when it is needed. However, Juan often plays with his son, but not so much with his daughters. The mother does not often play with the children. She has one strapped to her back and is constantly concerned about the others, but the children are expected to play with each other or to amuse themselves.

The children are not consciously instructed by either parent. The process is one of see and learn, without pressure from the parents to do so. The earlier aspects of socialization—toilet training, walking, speaking, sitting up—are considered by Roberta to unfold naturally without much aid from her. She keeps the child on her back until it is able to crawl. At about eighteen months she makes some effort to teach it to walk on her trips to the pila, on errands, or in the patio. At this age, the child is not expected to control its elimination. A child is led outside to eliminate in the patio, usually at the age of two and a half years, and when it begins to talk it is expected to announce its needs. Boys wear a woolen skirt rather than trousers until they are two or three years old, because they do not yet control elimination. Bed wetting and pants fouling is not taken seriously until five or six years of age, when parents begin to admonish children if it continues. At five or six the children begin to take up household tasks, aiding Roberta in the grinding of maize on a small *metate*, bringing water in a *tinaja* adjusted to the size of the girl, and in the care of her chickens. In Juan's family they will go to the factory school when they are six or seven.

The children are never encouraged by gifts or rewards for doing what is expected of them, but they are scolded or beaten, depending upon the gravity of the offense, for doing things the parents deem wrong. Children do not ask questions of their parents and rarely, in this household, seemed to exhibit the curiosity which we consider natural in growing children. We later found that the children were curious when they first shyly, and then more spontaneously, questioned us about many things, but they do not ask their parents who would think it troublesome. They learn by listening to scraps of conversation between adults and by watching adults behave. Most of the learning is in terms of what respect is due to whom and under what conditions; the only verbal instructions I have ever heard Juan and Roberta give, and the only kind they say they ever gave to their children, is that connected with salutations and obeisances in greeting elders and persons of respect. When children make a mistake in drawing inferences about behavior in a given situation, they are either reprimanded or struck lightly with the hand or with a leather whip. They are told that this action—for example, talking during meal time—is wrong and that they must not do it again. In extreme cases Roberta may try to frighten them as a mode of discipline; she may say, for example that the driver of the tractor on the highway under construction below the Pueblo would catch them if they misbehave again. Since the children are in contact with the mother during all the work day, they develop more confidence in her ability to estimate the extent and nature of a wrongdoing and to be judge of their achievement and to intercede with the father. They show a warmer response to the mother, and she shows them more affection. The children respond to the feelings of affection by being visibly more at ease in the household and with their parents than with any other set of adults, related or not.

Juan's children, though small, operate on the principle of age respect and male dominance. The boy, who is the youngest, is given special privileges within the household in regard to his sisters, and both he and his sisters take it as given that he is somewhat more important than they. In getting toys his preferences come first; he eats at the table with his father, while the girls squat with their mother. This works in conjunction with the age principle. The oldest girl takes care of her younger sister and brother, but she is much more permissive with the boy than with the girl. She sometimes gives advice and instruction to the younger girl on how to wear her clothing, how to carry a water jar, and how better to use the grinding stone. Toward the boy she is solicitous that he gets into no trouble and that he does not harm himself or disturb the mother's routine. To the sister, then, she has a relation of equivalence tempered with age superiority which makes the relationship one of slight authority. Toward the boy she has a relationship of subordination, modified by her advantage in years. This relationship is reflected in Juan's kinship terminology. He distinguishes brothers on the basis of older and younger brother, but sisters are not separated on the basis of age. The children use the same kind of kinship terms and have behavior closely fitted to those terms.

Like the factory worker, Reginio's center of kinship duty, familial loyalty, economic effort, and emotional life lies in the nuclear family.

Reginio is the center of respect and authority in the nuclear family. His wife express her subordination in the customary way of serving him first at meal times, by eating on the floor while he eats at the small table, and by attending to his wants before looking after her own. Reginio is theoretically the maker of familial decisions, and although he consults his wife for her opinion before arriving at any decision, his word is final. Should the decision be ill taken, his wife does not recriminate but considers it a stroke of bad fortune rather than as a decision she should have modified or insisted more strongly upon changing. The children are subordinate to both parents, and never talk back or countermand an order or suggestion. Instant, unquestioning obedience to parental demands is expected and usually received. Requests to children are usually given in an ordinary conversational voice and manner, and the children respond in the same rather casual way, slowly and without a hurry to show that the order has been complied with. The specificity of the authority roles makes the family a very easygoing one to the observer's eye, and the members themselves remark, when asked, that all goes smoothly without bickering or shouting.

The same sex and age factors operate among siblings in this family as in Juan's family. Age means respect, and maleness means more respect than femaleness. Older children are expected to share in household tasks. The young girl has a miniature water jar and a small broom and tiny grinding stone, modeled after her mother's, and uses them according to her ability in the actual performance of household tasks. The younger boy does not yet participate in the work in the field, but when he is about eight or nine, says Reginio, he will begin accompanying his father to the field with a smaller version of the hoe and a smaller net bag, to start his participation in the agricultural work.

There is a fairly strict division of labor between husband and wife in both families. Reginio is the worker in the milpa, the caretaker of the animals, and the provider of food. His wife runs the domestic sphere of meal preparation, cleaning and washing, water carrying, and tending the patio. The care of the children is mainly her responsibility, although Reginio participates by taking the children to town with him and by sitting at home with them when his wife is away. There are also tasks that both share: marketing in the plaza, selling corn and beans in the market, processing the corn after harvest, and carrying loads.

The labor is actually divided rather evenly, though the content of the male role is strikingly different. The woman dominates the domestic sphere, and the husband never enters unless the wife has some incapacitating illness and he cannot get other female help. The man works in the income-producing sphere, with the woman as a supplement in bringing food to him in the field or stripping corn or drying beans during the harvest seasons. In both households, the children share in miniature replicas of adult tasks insofar as they are able. The major difference is that the children of the factory worker go to school all day and will not be required to work at such an early age as will those of the farmer.

As a Consumption Unit

Family economics are largely in the hands of the male earner. Juan brings home his pay and gives his wife Q3 weekly for daily expenditures such as meat, sausage, and candles, which they both consider adequate to the running of the household. She may spend this money without any detailed explanation of what becomes of it, so long as the meals appear. Juan buys the corn, clothing, and larger items. Roberta must explain and justify any expenditure she makes or wants to make beyond her weekly allotment and the final vote is theoretically in Juan's hands, but in practice the decision is often made by Roberta and ratified by Juan. The only times Juan beats Roberta center around the expenditures she makes; at least this is the presumptive cause, and it happens only when he is drunk. In this he reflects the good husband in Cantel, who, it is said, beats his wife "solo por el gasto," only in matters of mismanagement or overspending of funds. The husband is usually correct in his suspicions. For the wife, as Roberta does, tries to save some money out of the weekly dole in order to buy something for herself. Roberta is unlike many of the wives who have a petty business of their own, but occasionally she, like many other women, sells small amounts of stored corn in order to purchase some item of clothing that she has long wanted but for which no money is forthcoming.

The family property is under the husband's control unless, like Roberta, the wife brings some property of her own to the marriage. Since it is customary for a woman not to merge her property with her husband's, she still has some land in her name. But assets accrued after marriage belong to the male and are his to use and dispose of during his lifetime. Of course, this is modified by exigency. That is, when the children are sick Juan may borrow money on his land if it is necessary to meet expenses, or he may do the same if his wife is ill. Property is held separately and thought of separately, if the wife has a clear right to some holdings or large items of her own, but her capital and the common lot are always under the control and management of the husband. Thus the pattern of household expenditures is determined within close limits by Juan's idea of a well run household. The savings are a function of what Juan saves and the goods accumulated are what Juan thinks worth accumulating.

Reginio the farmer, like Juan the factory worker, determines the income of the family by his management and labor in the fields and he gives his wife a more or less fixed sum each week to spend on household affairs, thereby determining the outgo. He purchases the larger items of consumption—clothing, utensils, household repairs, and so forth. His wife tells him when certain things are needed, but he decides if they can or will implement the need. Reginio's household expenditures match those of Juan in total outlay, and since their incomes are nearly commensurate their levels of living should be about the same. But the consumption pattern is different. Reginio's family spends less on clothing and medicine than does Juan's. The saving pattern is such that Reginio has a small edge on what he saves during a given year. Our figures on Reginio's household budgeting are not as complete as those for Juan, but an overall view seems to indicate that Juan tends to live up to the limit of his income more than does Reginio; Juan sometimes borrows money at interest from the local money-lenders, while Reginio tells me that he has no outstanding debts and manages to put something by almost every year. Reginio spends more for funerals than does Juan. He also has an outlay connected with the soul of his dead father—masses said in the latter's name, candles in the church, and flowers on the grave.

The similarity between Juan and Reginio comes in the way expenditure is controlled within the two families; the differences stem from the content of expenditure and the slight saving edge in the farm family.

As a Religious Center

The nuclear family has a house altar, which serves as a ceremonial or religious center. The saint which sits on the table in the sala, surrounded by flowers and with a candle or two in front of it, comes from Juan's family; it is his saint but serves to bless the whole family. The family prays to it as a unit only on the saint's day. There are daily prayers to be made to the saint, but that is each member's individual responsibility. Juan makes his obeisances alone in the morning, afternoon, and evening. Roberta, together with the children, offers the same set of prayers thrice daily. The schedule of prayer comes from the division of labor. The wife is in the kitchen preparing meals while the husband prays, and she must get Juan fed and off to work at a fixed time. In addition, there is the ideal that the relationship to the saint, or the saint's interest, depends upon the individual and that one should present himself for daily protection. The children pray along with the mother and learn the prayers, which she recites in Spanish.

The family goes to church as individuals; Juan rarely goes and Roberta takes the two oldest children on her rather infrequent visits. The family appears in church at baptisms and funerals. Juan served in the confradía system, which entailed a religious division of labor between him and his wife. He carried on the ceremonial aspects of prayer and care for the image, and she cooked for the assembled *cofrades* and helped wash the clothes of the brotherhood's saint. There is little common ceremonial activity or common religious sentiment in this family, except as it centers about the care of the house saint and the taking of precautions to insure the safety of the household and children. This is accomplished by such acts as putting some herb above the entrance to the house, by erecting a cross of maize in the drying corn after harvest, and other techniques which involve the cooperation of husband and wife.

Reginio's house saint, set up on a table in the sala, also comes from his father. The family does not worship it as a unit; each individual makes his thrice daily prayer to it alone, except that the younger children accompany the mother when she makes her prayers. The family works as a unit in religious or ceremonial life when it goes to mass together three times a year—on the fourth Friday of Easter, the fiesta titular, and on All Soul's Day. The religious well-being of the family is taken care of through the compliance of each of its members with the various tabus and prescribed behaviors current in the community as to an individual's relation with the supernatural. When Reginio served as a cofrade, of course, his wife was involved in the food-preparation and social-service aspects of that post. As in Juan's case, it is really a husband and wife who go through the office; the man discharges the overt aspects of the role and the woman provides the background. At harvest time the family places a maize cross in the corn drying in the patio as a thanks offering, and later saves the ears of corn which formed it to be placed on the house altar.

As religious units, the families are closely matched. The house altar is the family focus, and the devotions are carried on individually rather than collectively. The factory seems to have started neither a movement toward less home religion, nor toward greater group activity within the home. Both families carry on about the same set of rites and prayers: the saint in the main room, the maize cross at harvest time, the herb omen above the entrance, the house sacrifice when setting up a home, the thrice daily praying and lighting of candles, the silence during the meal which is considered to be like a mass, the familial attendance at mass on the three high holidays, and the wife's participation in the husband's religious post.

In the Compadrazgo System

A family extends its personal relations with others in the community through the *compadrazgo* system. By taking on ritual or fictional kin at life crises of baptism and marriage, they acquire a set of *padrinos* and *compadres* toward whom respect and deference is shown and from whom counsel may occasionally be expected. At his marriage Juan selected a couple he believed to be honorable and with whom none of his relatives had ever had a major dispute. He asked them to serve as padrinos of his marriage, and he and Roberta thereby acquired two older persons toward whom they would display and feel respect. When each of his children was born he asked couples nearer his own age to become padrinos to his children and thus compadres and comadres to him and his wife. He and his wife now have three sets of compadres, consisting of three separate couples, one set of padrinos through marriage, and the padrinos from their individual baptisms. There is a feeling of restraint between compadres, and they always greet each other by the appropriate respect term. The padrinos function as a weaker version of the biological uncle, giving advice and moral counsel. In Juan's life the compadre relationship is restricted largely to the formalized salutation when meeting and a somewhat greater concern about the fate of compadres than about a complete stranger. The compadres show some interest in their *ahijados*, but not much beyond providing what is required at the time the role is assumed.

The compadres take their tone from the vague and indefinite duties ascribed to consanguineal and affinal kin. They are less of a social resource and center of sentimental attachment than are real kin, but more so than unrelated persons. In a case of extreme need Juan will call on his compadres and he thinks they will probably respond. But his frequency of interaction is no greater with compadres than with non-compadres, and they seem to serve as a remoter form of insurance for his children should he for any reason be unable to mobilize members of his kindred for aid, or be unable to provide for them himself. Juan and Roberta, in their turn, take on compadre relationships when they are requested to. Juan is very popular and has more than 30 sets of ahijados and compadres, and he decides when the family shall take on the expense of providing clothing for a new-born child, when they shall pay a part of the marriage ceremony, and when they will accept compadre relationships. His choice is restricted by the desire not to accept offers from very close friends, for this means that the friendship would be terminated because of the substitution of respect relationships. He accepts offers from those with whom he has carried on minimal but amicable relations, and those who do not have outstanding disputes with him or with his wife's kinsmen. Being chosen as compadres is a ratification of the fact that Juan and Roberta are decent and respectable people, and that they do not become involved in personal feuding.

Reginio's assumption of fictional kindred through the compadre system is not especially wide. He has about five sets of compadres, who were chosen or chose him because there was neither a warm and intimate friendship nor an outstanding feud, and because all participants were considered steady and honorable persons. The compadre bonds entail respect and special terms of greeting when compadres meet. They do not lead to much increased interaction, to the borrowing or lending of money, or to the exchange of work in the field. Reginio sometimes uses the *dar mano* or labor exchange in harvesting or planting his fields, and when he needs unpaid outside help he goes to the neighbors with whom he has worked out a set of reciprocal work days in their respective fields. He does not utilize either kinship or compadrazgo in this, but prefers a business-like quid pro quo exchange of labor time, picking men whose work is about equivalent to his own in skill and productivity.

In summary, then, the families are almost identical kinds of groupings with respect to their relations with kindred, their internal structure, their economic aspect, the means of authority and control, division of labor, and home religion. The differences are apparent in lessened economic dependence upon the household head's father, and in the role of the younger generation. The family itself has had to make no behavioral or sentimental adjustment to the fact that its chief earner derives his income from a nontraditional and recently introduced occupational role.

The generalization that the factory worker's family has undergone no cycle of change which makes it diverge from nonfactory families, as based upon the foregoing comparison, is capable of being extended to the generality of factory families where the chief earner is head of the household. The generalization thus established holds that factory families are, within the social and cultural variability common to family organization in Cantel, like farm families in their social arrangements and cultural understandings.

OTHER FAMILY UNITS

This comparison of families is only a partial answer to the problem of the differentiation of the factory worker's familial relationships. The complete answer needs an analysis of kinds of families—specifically, the family in which a son or daughter is a factory worker but lives at home; the family in which both husband and wife are factory workers; the family in which the woman is a factory worker and the man is not; and finally the family arrangements in which young persons are maintaining their parents in the children's domicile. These other family units are those in which the strains generated by factory employment upon traditional arrangements may be most clearly seen.

My discussion of them emphasizes the control mechanisms which prevent the strains from crystallizing into new social forms. The proposition to which I subscribe is that the tensions of family life continue to be suppressed by traditional means of social control, but these tensions in part provide the basis for institutional changes which came in the wake of the 1944–54 decade of revolution. To be fully explicit: factory work subjects the family to a series of new opportunities for emotional and social organization, but these paths are not taken unless a major shift occurs in the distribution of local political power, as happened in Cantel through the organization of the union. My thesis on the family stresses its long-time defensive ability in a social situation of continual pressure—pressure which found its outlet in the backwash of national political ferment as that was channelized by the local union.

Unmarried Daughter or Son Employed in Factory

When an unmarried son or daughter works in the factory and lives at home, there is a common mechanism for maintaining the authority and respect relations between a child and the parents. Factory personnel who live at home show the same deference to their parents as do their nonfactory counterparts. The explanation for this appears to lie in the control of family income and in the ownership and responsibility of the house site and its management. Farmers' children who work in the factory turn over their entire income to the parents, with almost no exception if the occasional withholding of a few pennies be discounted. Those to whom I have talked tell me that they turn over the money because it is a duty—that when one lives in his parents' household, he is under their rule. The head of the household is the controller of all funds coming into and going out of the household; the children turn over their income to him because they consider him to be in the role of provider and manager of the household in which they are only residents. The head of the household can enforce this definition of the role by the ultimate sanction of denying the children access to the household unless they accede to the working rules. Since most young earners cannot establish separate households until they are married and able to afford to buy or build a house, the simple lack of alternative is a great deterrent to revolt against parental authority. Furthermore, the absence of restaurants or rentable units, combined with the stigma of living *recomendado*—in someone else's home, when you have a family—sets additional limits upon alternatives to living at home. The friction between young workers and their parents is alleviated by the head of the household allowing the child to purchase many more personal items than would customarily be permitted.

The situation for daughters who work in the factory is much the same. Their income and expenditure pattern is determined by the head of the household in which they live, and on the same grounds of duty combined with sanction which leave no recourse. Since a woman may neither engage in active courting nor in overt demands for independence or marriage, some factory girls have established residences in which two or more "career" girls set up their own households. This is usually done only when the parents are dead and the factory girl does not want to live with another relative. It is a deviant pattern in Cantel, and the deviancy is recognized by the girls, who accept it as a necessary and transitory solution. Such girls are often talked about as being unwilling to take on the job of housewife, implying that they are only partial women. Less than one percent of single factory girls live in this way, and it shows no signs of becoming more prevalent. Its importance lies in the possibility which the free use of factory income affords for household composition. It is not more subversive of the going family structure because it has no moral sanction and is impermanent in nature.

Both Husband and Wife Employed in the Factory

When both the husband and wife are factory workers (there are 64 such cases among Indians and 5 among Ladinos), another problem is posed for the traditional family. Equality of earning and of economic control is absent from the normal Cantelense family. A wife who earns money outside their joint labors customarily considers that money hers, as does her husband. Women often, but not always, turn over some or all of their income from minor economic activities, chiefly embroidery or sewing, to the common household fund. They can and do keep for themselves what they deem just and use these funds in any manner they see fit, usually for clothing or adornment. Generally, this income is of the "pin money" class and would not significantly alter the total household assets. But the factory wife earns a larger income, the free disposition of which would give her economic independence and personal sufficiency normally beyond both the reach and aspiration of Cantel women. The problem posed by a wife working in the factory turns about the social implications of this economic position, with its possibilities for a more equalitarian husband-wife relationship and a more equal share in the disposal of family income; taken together, these contain the possibility of modifying the cultural consensus on family sentiment.

As might be expected, the families in which this problem occurs have adjusted in a number of idiosyncratic ways, none of which is equalitarian between husband and wife or blurs the authority relation between them. The most common arrangement is for the wife to turn over to her husband almost all of her income, keeping back a small amount over which she has control. This kind of handling gives the husband the same control over domestic economy as if his wife were not a factory employee earning a rather large income. I am unable to say definitely whether or not the husband's authority is in this instance diminished, but it appears not to be in the one case I know intimately. Despite the wife's voluntary surrender of an income equal in size to the husband's, he does not reciprocate by allowing her a greater share in decision making and she does not assert her rights to equality of status within the family. This appears to be the general case, judging by the fact that wives so employed do not leave their husband's household with any greater, and possibly with less, frequency than do nonfactory women. But marriage, as in other Mesoamerican communities, is highly brittle. Turning over most of the money to the husband is accepted as the duty and normal behavior of a wife; so long as the husband does not squander money on things such as drink, the arrangement brings what is considered a fair return and makes for a happier family because it is not beset by the many financial difficulties which plague the usual set of spouses.

In ten cases, the factory-employed wife and her spouse live in her natal household. Under these conditions it is customary for her to split her income between her parents and her husband, on the theory that she has a divided duty—one to her parents for still being under their roof, and one to her husband as the head of the separate household.

Like nonfactory ones, factory women do not consider themselves exploited if they work and turn over their income to the husband or father. They receive a greater share in material expenditure than they would if they were not factory workers. The factory woman is better off than the nonfactory woman in terms of her material possessions and in the quality of her clothing, and much better off than if she did not work. She is also culturally similar to the nonfactory women in being able to carry out the other requirements of womanhood in Cantel, and therefore regards herself as a woman who is better off and is so regarded by other women in the society. She is of course regarded as an asset to the family or husband with whom she is associated. Many factory women, whose husbands are also employed in the factory, work for definite purchases such as a house, and their work time is therefore limited.

Parents Dependent Upon Factory-Employed Child

Because of factory income there are often sons or young men who are richer and economically more secure than their parents or elders. Where the father or mother is supported in the child's home, the case is most likely to be one in which the child is a factory worker. This support of parents by young factory-employed children reverses former dependency relations and violates cultural expectations. It is different from the agricultural instances, which usually result from the father giving the son the house and land upon which the father will later be supported. The factory child is supporting poor parents on the returns from his own economic effort, and often without any economic gifts from the parents.

In these families, the parent or parents are given the respect and deference due them because of their kinship category, but they are stripped of authority and power by the circumstance of being under a roof kept by others. The older persons do not control the family exchequer of these households or determine the consumption and expenditure pattern of their children. The normal role of the parent vis-á-vis his children is segmented: the respect and deference components are split off from the economic control and personal authority aspects. There is some discomfort in a role thus divided, but the child tends to say he is complying with his duty toward his parents, and the parents remark that the children are good because they have taken on this burden of support. Nonetheless, this type of family is subversive of the operating relationships between parents and children, between age and youth, and should agriculture deteriorate economically while the factory held its own, it might by increased incidence cause significant changes in the overall family picture of Cantel.

From the description of the family in Cantel as related to the occupational role of factory worker, it becomes clear that the fact of being so employed has not to any great extent created new family structures or emotional patterns. The families of factory workers are remarkably similar in form and content to those of nonfactory workers. The major divergences seem to lie in two directions. First, the greater economic resource of the factory family, in relation to the prevailing income structure of Cantel, promotes the integration of the nuclear family by resolving some of the tensions associated with disposal of very limited means. Second, the factory worker takes on the support of his parents, should the need arise, at an early age and under conditions formerly absent from the community. These divergences have not so differentiated the factory worker from the farmer that great and socially visible, and possibly friction-producing, disparities in their respective social lives are apparent. The factory worker continues to realize the cultural expectations of his society in the character of his familial existence.

That the differences are not greater nor the occupational role more disruptive appears to stem from the evolution of constraining mechanisms within the family as to the disposal of income earned by factory workers. These mechanisms, combined with the importance of household ownership and the conception of duty while living under someone's roof, indicate one set of responses which are empirically capable of containing pressures generated by new sources of income and by a different distribution of earners. At the same time, these mechanisms cover the strains which if left unresolved are the probable roots of such family disruption in many industrializing under-developed areas.

FRIENDSHIP AND VOLUNTARY ASSOCIATIONS

It is to the friendship and associational bonds, to which we now turn, that one may look for growing differentiation between factory and nonfactory personnel because of their economic activity.

Absence of a Tradition of Friendship

Customary behavior in Cantel does not include visiting friends and relatives, except upon strictly defined occasions. There is no activity which corresponds to our notion of the casual social visit, nor is there any concept which approximates our view of leisure time and recreational activity. The streets of the Pueblo are nearly deserted after the working day, and in each house the nuclear family spends its time alone without thought of visitors or of visiting. In the rural cantones the situation is duplicated. After eight o'clock in the evening the municipio seems to be a deserted town, except for the dull lights which glint through the night haze in the village and the slightly stronger street lights of the factory. No one is about, unless it be a drunk shouting in the streets or the hourly vigil of the night watch, which begins after midnight.

A woman calls on another in terms of an errand provoked by necessity, some impelling need to seek a neighbor's company such as the buying or selling of a small item, the borrowing or lending of money, or the carrying of food in time of illness. The idle visit to exchange pleasantries is culturally prohibited, and gossip and the counsel given at marriage back these prohibitions. If a woman visits for pleasure, as she often does, it must be couched in the rationalization, plausible to both visitor and hostess, of some urgent and impersonal reason for seeking a neighbor's company during the time when there is work to do. During the work week, men are either in their fields, at their special occupations, or in the factory. They neither have nor find the time to engage in social visiting during these hours.

In keeping with this, and perhaps because of it, there does not appear to be a pattern of friendship relationships in our sense of the word. People do not develop deep and intimate relations with nonkinsmen. There are no opportunities in the ordinary life for protracted personal interaction with nonkinsmen, nor any associational structures based upon the premise of like interests or upon ideas of fellowship or sport. The non-kin groupings which are part of the traditional society, such as the religious associations of the local catholic church or the voluntary religious societies of folk catholicism, do not provide a mode or place for the intimate and prolonged social interaction which alone may develop into the personal understandings necessary for friendship in the Western sense. The temporary grouping of men into civil or religious offices, such as the cofradías or the group of young civil police who serve for a year, is so stylized and custom controlled in most of its aspects that personal knowledge of the individuals with whom one serves is nearly impossible. In those aspects where custom does not provide formal mechanisms for personal interaction, such as in the exchange of cofradías or in the relief of office at the end of a term, alcoholic excess is always the case. Alcohol serves to bridge the gap when personal reactions are called for but there are no grounds for them.

Women are also in the same circumstances. They are thrown together on a non-kin basis only under short and impersonal

circumstances. At fiestas or where they are the female counterparts
of male exchange of office, they too use alcoholic excess as a means
of overcoming tensions in personal situations and of preventing
the situation from becoming one which demands coherent
personal responses. In these situations, drinking is licensed
behavior.

Formation of Friendships in the Factory

Such lack of friendship bonds or of associational or special
action structures still characterizes the farming and artisan
population of the municipio. Factory workers diverge from this
pattern in participating in associational and voluntary organizations, and in having perduring relations of friendship. The fact
that friendships are formed chiefly among factory workers relates
to two sources in their occupational role. First, the situation within
the factory requires association of nonkinsmen for long periods,
and the work requires some kind of personal communication in
carrying it out. Second, the formation of a union based upon
common interest and democratic election procedure and control,
provided an associational structure which permitted the growth
of personal interactions and offered grounds for the cultivation
of personal relations which may eventuate in friendship. Furthermore, other voluntary groups oriented toward leisure activity
have grown up around the factory nucleus—a soccer team, a bicycle
club, and a now defunct basketball team. As an example of how
such friendships develop, Juan Q. has made two close friends in
factory work. He works in the spinning department where there is
a minimum of necessary communication between workers on the
same machine line and between workers and the caporal who over-
sees them. Juan has become friends with two of the men on his line.
The friendships are now of long standing, and although he and one
of his friends have been up-graded to caporal since the formation
of his two alliances, he is still friendly with the man who was not
up-graded. Juan describes the formation of relationships with
these men as being due to working together. They talked to one
another about the common job of working the machine, the things
that controlled output, the state of wages and hours, and similar
small details of their common experience on the job. Soon they
found themselves walking away from work together at the end of
the day, or seeking each other out for a chat during lunch hour.
Over the years they became more intimate, using first name

salutations when greeting, a form generally used between an adult and a child or between kinsmen of rather close degree.

When the union was in the process of formation, Juan and his two friends were much thrown together and given another set of common and specific experiences to share, which, according to Juan, deepened their love for each other. They began to invite each other to visit their homes on Sundays and on festal occasions, where only kin and sometimes neighbors were usually invited. Their wives became acquainted on these Sunday visits and their children played together, reinforcing the men's friendship links. When Juan drinks now, he usually does not drink alone but seeks out one of his friends; or they seek him out. He and the other two men speak of each other as friends, a socially different designation from the agricultural Cantelense's reference to all nonkin as either acquaintance or nonacquaintance, or by spatial reference to a near or far neighbor.

This is the classic kind and extent of friendship relation which has developed from the occupational role of worker. Some things about it are notable. The friendship bond does not proliferate beyond the nuclear family. Beyond the work place, friendship still waits upon invitation for prolonged social interaction, which is restricted to Sundays and festal occasions. The families of the men are necessarily involved in this relationship, and compatibility must be established between their wives if the relationship is to flourish. Village status considerations play no part in the formation or continuance of a friendship, and the different authority positions on the job are no hindrance to its formation. If the friendships are job-formed, they are with those immediately connected with the work; spinner befriends spinner, weavers get to know weavers, and machine workers extend bonds with machine workers. To my knowledge, there is no case of a friendship formed in the factory which extended across departmental lines. The differences from our own friendship pattern are obvious, but the basis for forming friendships is similar to ours in that they revolve on a core of shared experiences and develop among a group assembled for functionally specific reasons.

Stimulation of Friendship Bonds in the Union

The factory appears to be the kind of associational structure which is most conducive to the generation of bonds of personal and intimate connection beyond the definition of blood and marriage ties. The formation of the factory workers' union gave rise to an organization which also operated on principles of personal contact not present in the prefactory society. In the process of organization, men who were already personally familiar with each other because of factory-formed friendships, attempted to recruit Canteleños into the organization on the basis of ideological commitment, stressing personal loyalties both to the idea of unionization and to the individuals who would form the membership of the union. This kind of appeal had very limited success. But the union's success in winning material and economic advances attracted most of the factory workers into an organization committed to the collective ideology of democratic unionism and to person-to-person bonds of loyalty and solidarity to promote the social realization of the idea.

Those individuals within the union who carried on the executive and administrative functions often formed friendships. But also, within the membership at large, conditions of interaction around common problems necessitated intimate communication about work and wages, with its concomitant of risk and danger to the continuity and conditions of employment; this provided fertile soil for the evaluation of people as individuals and for the growth of sentimental and affectual ties between them.

The union and the factory supplied the situational basis for the formation of friendships, and friendships are almost without exception confined to those who have been through these social experiences. But in addition, the union, the factory, the sport clubs—all restricted to factory employees—provided new bases for association and new kinds of social experience even for those who, for some reason, did not form friendship relations.

The growth of a special action structure based on common interest and buttressed by friendship ties is a change of magnitude. Its full effect is not seen in the personal lives of participants, but in the shifting basis of social and political power which will be treated in the section on institutional modifications.

6

Religious Life and World View: A Comparison of the Practices and Beliefs of Factory and Farm Worker

I NOW direct attention to comparison of a few remaining aspects of the factory worker's life with the nonfactory worker's; namely, in the spheres of religion and belief, and in world view. Religious life and its accompanying symbolic content and social component may be conveniently divided into three parts: (1) organized Christian experience, (2) Folk Catholicism, and (3) esoteric beliefs. Each part of the whole religious life has an analytically distinct content and structure.

ORGANIZED CHRISTIAN EXPERIENCE

The Catholic religion is the most formal; it is represented in the municipio by the church building and by the priest, resident in Cantel for more than 10 years. The Church nominally operates according to the dogma and ritual of the Roman Church. As extensions of its spiritual business it maintains two secular organizations in Cantel, the *Acción Católica Cantel* and *Madres Cristianas*. For the proclaimed Catholics, the Church regulates the rites de passage of baptism, marriage, and death. The images are housed in the church edifice where masses are said and private orations offered. The Church observes holidays and festal days according to Roman edict, adding and emphasizing Spanish and Spanish-American holidays and observances. Much of what is considered important by the priest and his informed followers, the *catequistes*—those who know the catechism—is not part of the local variety of Catholic belief and ritual. For example, while I was in Cantel it was Marian Year, according to the Holy See, but no special observance or devotions to Mary were carried out, nor were many aware that such were called for in all Catholic communities. For our purposes, then, we may consider the Catholic Church of Cantel as an organization whose ostensible purpose is to bring Catholic precept and morality to bear in local life. This is carried out by a resident priest with the aid of a paid assistant and several voluntary helpers. The other personnel of the Church are the *fiscales*, appointed through the civil-religious hierarchy, who keep the Pueblo's church and care for the vestments of the images housed in the church. The local Church is related to the Catholic hierarchy via the bishop of Quezaltenango, who makes periodic visits to the village and transmits instructions to the priest. Beyond this level of authority, the relations of the local Church fade into the remoter vistas of the hierarchy, without observable social effect in Cantel.

The other area of organized Christian experience is represented by the four Protestant groups in the community. Three are of North American derivation, and one of Guatemalan origin. They are Presbyterian, Seventh Day Adventist, Pentecostal, and *Cramerista*, the Guatemalan derivative of the Plymouth Brethren. All have physical plants, more or less elaborate private houses converted into temples. Only the Presbyterians have a locally resident pastor, a Cantelense, who earns his living in that capacity. The others depend for pastoral guidance upon outsiders resident in Quezaltenango, Momostenango, or Guatemala City, but they have local leaders in the sense of nonordained heads of the congregation who carry out the details and duties which give these organizations local continuity. No one is sure exactly how many Protestants there are in the municipio, due to only partial commitment by some of those who attend Protestant churches. The best count I could get, based on reported membership by the Protestants themselves and on the Catholic priest's counteroffensive to Protestantism, is between 450 and 500 Protestants in the entire municipio. The largest group is the Presbyterian, next the Cramerista, then the Adventist, and finally the Pentecostal. For the Protestants, their sect officiates at the marriage, baptism, and death rites, and also gives classes in religious instruction. The Adventists run a primary school in the village, attended by both Adventists and non-Adventists. The striking difference between the Protestant Churches and the Catholic Church is of course the doctrine of voluntary ingress. In Cantel this manifests itself in continual supervision of the daily conduct of a member of a Protestant sect by his brethren to ascertain whether he behaves in conformity with the spirit of the cult. Negatively, this means giving up certain minor personal vices such as smoking, drinking, and the public use of swear words; positively, it means adoption of close ties to other members of the cult, using the term "brother," more friendly attitudes toward strangers, and the duty to expound the creed to whomever will listen.

FOLK CATHOLICISM

The second major division of religious life in Cantel may be called Folk Catholicism. There is no folk element to Protestantism, since its practices are always under supervision by the membership for conformity to conscious and prescribed creed and practice. Folk Catholicism refers to those aspects of religious belief and practice which have grown up around the core of Catholic rite and dogma, as the people of Cantel have for more than four centuries adapted parts of the formal workings of the Catholic Church to their local needs and understandings. It is the spontaneous growth of the interaction of a small Indian society with an aspect of a civilized tradition. As such, many of its elements are of Catholic origin, some are of pagan derivation, and many are an outgrowth of the dynamics of these two systems working upon each other. But as a contemporary social entity or cultural complex, it is a new thing, not resolvable into the strains which gave it birth. In Cantel, Folk Catholicism is the largest and most important part of the religious life of the people. For many it is almost all of the religious life, but for all except Protestants it is the core of supernatural belief and technique.

Religious societies are one element of the folk religion. Thirteen religious societies function more or less independently but with the approval of the Catholic Church, and each one is dedicated to the adoration of a particular saint. These societies are democratic in membership and leadership. A man becomes a member voluntarily, depending upon his predilection for one or another of the roster of saints. The officers of any given society are chosen by the members after indicating their willingness to undertake the care and housing of the image (in some cases only a large portrait of the saint). The societies sometimes merge if there are not enough members in a certain year, or if no one wants to undertake responsibility. Members often change from one society to another, and at different periods in Cantel history one society may be more popular than another. The essential characteristic of these societies is their dependence upon the current state of devotion and popularity accorded a given saint. They represent the fashionable aspect of Catholic-derived religion.

The religious rite associated with the saint merges in importance with the secular display in these societies. The person who undertakes the *cargo*, the job of caring for the image that year, gives a feast upon his ritual reception into office, and the elaborateness and luxury of this feast, plus the outlay in new clothing for the saint, is as much a status-conferring device as a religious exercise. The cargo is usually undertaken because the person has requested and received some favor from the saint, and this is his manner of showing gratitude. But in the most popular societies, *Justo Juez* and *Soledad*, there is keen competition for the post. Expenses are large—running up to Q200 and Q300 for the reception—and the social honor at getting such a post is very great. Lesser societies may discharge their exchanges of office for as little as Q20, and there is little honor or competition for these posts. The rites at any exchange of saints are a garbled version of Spanish and Latin prayers, usually conducted by a *cantor*, a man versed in chanting either Spanish or Latin hymns and prayers who performs for a small fee. The important element in society ritual is not the strict compliance with stylized behavior, although that is a part of the ceremony attendant upon the saint; it is the presence of voluntary disciples who show their devotion to the saint and bid him confer upon them those blessings within his power, since each saint has peculiar virtues and is best able to manipulate certain areas of the supernatural according to his inherent virtues.

The second element in Folk Catholicism is the system of religious brotherhoods, the cofradías. These operate in conjunction with the civil administration of the municipio, and it does some violence, which I shall attempt to repair later, to treat them in their religious dimension only. The cofradías operate with the tacit consent and grudging approval of the Catholic Church. Of late there has been conflict between the cofradías and the Church over certain practices held to be in violation of dogma, but the friction is seldom apparent and leads to conflict only when the Church attempts to suppress or intervene in the activities of the cofradías. The cofradías do not now have formal status in the Church, although some 15 years ago they carried on functions at regular mass and other Catholic rituals under the care of the priest. There are seven cofradías, divided in common parlance and in fact into three large ones and four smaller ones. The former are larger in membership and greater in religious importance, therefore more honor is derived from serving in them.

Each cofradía is organized about a particular saint, and the job of the cofrades, as the incumbents of the brotherhood are called, is the care of this saint. This care includes the proper devotions, celebrations of the saint's day, marching in the processions, having mass said at the proper time, keeping the cofradía stocked with candles, incense, and clothing for the saint, and preserving and repairing the image itself. The rites are traditional and carried on by men appointed for the year's services.

In effect, the cofradías are corporations in perpetuity, with the effects of the corporation belonging to the saint and being passed on each year to different persons whose job it is to carry out the duties of being officers of the corporation. Unlike the devotion and care provided the saints of the societies, the duty of being a cofrade is a public one; it involves the delegation of sacred duties by the community to certain members, eligible by age and previous service for these communal chores. The staff of any cofradía is named each year by the *Comité de Organizador de Cofradías* from a listing of those families who have not served recently or whose turn is due, in the opinion of the committee. This nomination was formerly made by municipal authority at the recommendation of the principales, the village elders, who had served in the top posts of either the civil or religious branches of the hierarchy. Now a man may refuse to serve when he is called to cofrade duty, but refusal is still somewhat rare. The cofradías function without formal clerical help.

Basically, the cofradías contain an informal arrangement of Catholic rite and litany combined with folk imputation to the saints of special provinces or power. Of course, there are minor observances which are Indian elements outside of European Catholic practice, and in some cases peculiar to Cantel—the slowness of walking in a procession which denotes respect; the rocking of the saint before bringing the image into a house; the lighting of the daily candle; the hanging of wax figures around the saints when asking certain favors; the tapping on the saint's foot with a coin before offering a prayer; and the burning of incense with offerings. But the social importance of the cofradía system lies in the fact that the whole village is related to the saints and the supernatural through its appointed delegates, and that personal activity or devotion is not required of individuals for the proper homage and maintenance of harmonious relations with the sacred. In the ideal functioning of the system, each family does its duty when its turn comes up; meantime, its welfare is being

taken care of by those now serving the saints and _Díos_ in its name
and with its sanction.

The cofradía system is thus a pivotal aspect of communal religion, and the more so since it enters into the age and prestige
stratification of the village as it operates in conjuction with the
civil hierarchy. The term costumbre, denoting the traditional
behavior of the people taken as self-evidently necessary and self-
justifying, is used mainly in reference to the cofradías and their
practices. The organized Church directs some hostility toward the
cofradías because from its viewpoint their Catholicism is irregular,
and because the system rather than the formal doctrine and practice
of the Church is the strong point of religious allegiance.

ESOTERIC BELIEFS

The third significant element in the religious life of Cantel can be
discussed under the rubric of esoteric beliefs. I use this title for
those practitioners who are not organized into any social group,
but who form a category of men and women possessing occult
knowledge of sacred character and to whom the society as a whole
ascribes powers and techniques of contact and communication
with a set of supernatural elements. Cantelenses believe in this
segment of the supernatural.

The practitioners of these esoteric beliefs and techniques are
of two kinds, _ʔaxʔiȼ_, the caster of evil spells, and _ʔaxʔix_, the diviner
and maker of costumbre and sometimes medical specialist. The
general term covering all esoteric specialists is _chimán_ or _sanjorin_,
which I shall use, since no one in the village claims the ability to
perform the deadly magic of _ʔaxʔiȼ_, though all the chimanes know
how it is done and probably do it. The esoteric religion centers
about the 260-day divinatory calendar of the ancient Maya, and
each chimán uses the 20 day gods and the 13 number system in
combination with the "beans" and quartz crystals as the core of his
ritual. The believers in this system, or more properly the clients
of the chimanes, do not form any special grouping or have other
permanent relations to the chimanes except that of clients and
patients. A person brings his request to the chimán—be it interpretation of a dream, diagnosis of an illness, request for a fortune,
or prediction of the immediate future—performs the rites, and
pays the fee entailed in his particular case. No man makes his
living by being such a practitioner. There also centers around the
chimanes a complex of belief in "owners of the hills," special

places of great sacredness and great danger, which will be treated in the section on world view.

Included in the esoteric religion is the image called "San Simon" or "Judas." This image, housed in the permanent dwelling place of one of the cofradías, is a Ladino figure of straw, adorned with a wooden mask, a painted black mustache, and sunglasses. "San Simon" is an "escondido," an image not open to public view. It is regarded as the locus of the black powers of the devil, but it can be appealed to for special favors and grants. Its worship is on a payment basis and of a voluntary nature. Its ritual is one of burning copal (never used in the church or in the cofradías or societies) and saying certain Quiché invocations not derived from the Folk Catholic stream.

I have listed the religious divisions of Cantel without showing their functional integration and points of contact and friction, which I reserve for treatment in the section on cultural and institutional modification. I list them in order to discuss the nature of factory-worker and farmer participation in and subscription to them, and to ascertain if such differences as appear may be attributed to the special occupational role of the factory worker.

COMPARISON OF THE FARMER AND FACTORY WORKER IN RELIGIOUS ACTIVITIES

In the Catholic Church

The factory worker shows the same kind and degree of religious participation in the Catholic Church and its related secular organizations as does the nonfactory worker. Men customarily do not attend church unless there is some private reason such as a life crisis, or some public ritual which requires their presence. Some 40 to 50 men appear to be the regular communicants at mass, along with 80 to 100 women. These are the handful of local Catholics who have immersed themselves in the faith, together with those few who are carrying out some kind of *novena* or penance, usually self-imposed through a traditional definition of religious duty. This group of regular churchgoers is about proportionately divided among the occupational categories in Cantel, and appears to bear no relationship to such categories. Workers and nonworkers are socially equivalent in their attention or inattention to Catholic religious activity. In the other formal categories of the Church, such as the

sacraments and tithing, there appears some difference. Factory
workers have proportionately more church weddings than do nonfactory workers, because of their ability to bear the expense. This
indicates only the greater incidence of realization of a common
cultural end on the part of the factory man, rather than a modification of such ends. As for baptism and burial, all Cantelenses who
are Catholic go through these rites. Confession is rare, except at
the deathbed, and according to the two padres who were in the
parish during my stay, only a handful of persons confess regularly.
In this handful are some factory workers.

In belief and knowledge of the doctrine and creed of the Catholic
Church, workers show the same strengths and weaknesses as does
the larger population. For both, belief means acknowledgment
of the primacy of Christ and the saints in the supernatural world;
it does not entail a knowledge of or subscription to the official
doctrines and creeds of the organized Church, nor is it taken to
place great restriction upon the range of personal behavior or to
require any further moral commitments. The morality of the
community may be constructed as sacred, but the quality of sacredness lies outside of the formal teachings of the Catholic Church.
The commonest elements of Catholic belief in this community—
purgatory, paradise, the divinity of Christ, the Virgin Mary cult,
and the baptism—are taken at face value by those who hold them.

All Catholics share beliefs in the same roster of saints, attribu-
ting to each saint the local definition of his miraculous power; all
participate in the same festal calendar celebrating the religious
days in the sacred year; all can list the same sins, even if they are
not in the venal and mortal categories; all can repeat the Lord's
Prayer, Hail Mary, and Credo, taking these to be the chief litanies
and expressions of faith. There is no need to detail further the
elements of belief common to the Cantelenses. The point to be
made is patent: culturally considered, belief and understanding
of the formal aspects of Catholic religion are uniform; those who
are Catholic are so to the same degree of strength and with the same
kind of faith. The faith may not be a whole cloth of Roman religion,
nor of a burning intensity, but it accords well with the local view
of the supernatural. This consistency of belief as one goes from
worker to farmer is not a cause for wonder, nor a thing that merits
explanation. The uniformity stems from the fact that no new
sources of Catholic belief and doctrine have come to inject dis-
cordant or different beliefs, and the people do not invent new

ones. So it is that those who are Catholic are Catholic in the same way, and the belief system of their Catholicism is then a cultural element to which one either subscribes or does not subscribe.

The Church, under the resident priest, has waged intermittent war on the cofradía system of Folk Catholicism. But this is a negative kind of warfare to turn people away from the cofradías and toward the Church for their religious expression and allegiance, telling them of the thing that the cofradías do which are not part of the sanctioned practice of Catholicism. This attack does not modify the formal content of the Church religion, nor does it modify the content of the cofradía system, since the cofrades persist in their beliefs and practices with or without the blessing of the local representatives of the Church. It has modified the power relationships between the two aspects of Catholic faith, and perhaps slivered off some of the pesonnel available for cofradía service, but its effects in bringing cofradía belief and practice into compliance with official doctrine have been nil.

In the Protestant Sects

Workers have turned toward Protestantism with less frequency than have farmers or artisans.

From the census taken of the three settlement areas and from the membership rolls of the Protestant churches, it appears that Protestantism is most attractive to artisans, many of whom are Ladinos or "Ladinoized" Indians, for 10 percent of factory families, 13.5 percent of farm families and 17.9 percent of the artisan families are Protestants. Protestantism is the religion of the marginal man, when viewed from the perspective of the whole community. The embracing of Protestantism entails the re-formation of personal habits—the elimination of drinking, smoking, wife-beating, and generally lax behavior. Cantelenses who feel the desire to reform are those who for some reason are not at ease in their social and cultural environment. The comparative rarity with which workers turn toward Protestantism is an indication that factory employment is not of itself a source of stress.

In the Factory Church

Only one aspect of the Catholic religion may be said to belong almost exclusively to the workers and thus be attributed to the introduction of the factory. In the settlement of factory workers near the plant there is a religious subcommunity centered about the modern church edifice erected by the company. Mass is celebrated in this church every Sunday afternoon. Attendance here is not much greater than at the morning mass in the village church, but it is chiefly factory workers who come to this mass, and among these, mainly women or wives of factory men. The church and its activities make no striking deviation, although they do give the workers some religious separatism.

The factory community has its own unofficial patron saint. St. Anthony, an image given to some factory workers by an empleado long since gone from the community, is considered by the factory settlement to be its patron and special saint. This gives the factory workers' community symbolic distinctness from the other segments of the society. However, it is not distinctness of a divergent kind. Other settlements within the municipio—for example, Estancia with its Esquipulas saint images—have their local symbols and a degree of symbolic separateness. But all settlements and their populations are under the symbolic ascendancy of the patron saint of the entire municipio, *La Virgen de los Angeles*.

The factory workers organize an annual celebration in honor of their patron saint. This fiesta is financed by voluntary contributions from factory workers, since there is here no organization of cofradías to undertake the expense and handling of such an enterprise. A committee is appointed each year from among the members of the factory community to arrange the entire affair. There are always men willing to serve in this capacity, for the factory workers of the settlement are very fond of San Antonio.

The importance of this religious cult lies in the fact that by means of a mystical symbol it organizes and integrates into a social community both native born Cantelenses and resident foreigners who are living in a set of spatial arrangements determined by the requirements of centralized factory production. For Cantelenses this society does not occasion a transfer of major symbolic allegiance, but only a local focusing; for non-Cantelenses it provides a community of symbols with the strangers among whom they must live. The St. Anthony aspect of factory religion is best understood, I think, not as a change in the nature of religious belief, but as a proliferation of such belief and its concomitant symbolic and integrative devices.

In the Societies of the Saints

The factory population participates in the societies of saints, as does the nonfactory population. In the religious societies of which I have knowledge, workers join with a frequency equal to that of nonworkers. In the more popular societies, there are more workers just as there are more farmers. However, workers have modified these societies. Some members claim that it is they who have in recent years increased the lavish expenditure on the reception of the cargo of a saint. Farmers or farm workers have maintained this tradition, and the current manner of receiving the care of a saint therefore involves a great display of expenditure, and public recognition and approval of the lavishness as a sign of intensity of devotion and as a benchmark from which to accord social honor. In addition, members who work in the factory have modified the three-day home display of the image prior to the procession through the streets. The modification is usually minor, but connected to the fact of industrial technology, as in the case of the image of Christ called Justo Juez. This image was decorated with a series of light bulbs around the crown and on its wooden platform, instead of the usual candles. This wiring of the image was done by a Cantelense who was an electrician in the factory electric shop.

For all prayers and ceremonies connected with the yearly exchange of the saint, the same rituals are carried out whether or not the partners to the exchange include a factory worker, and irrespective of the number of factory workers or farmers who happen to be members of the society. The religious societies have not changed in content, number, or associated belief because some of the members are now industrial employees.

In the Cofradías

In the carrying out of religious belief, it is primarily in folk aspects that differentiation between factory and nonfactory worker appears, although that divergence is not great. As of 1954, there are six cofradías operating in Cantel. Seven such brotherhoods are organized, and in the minds of the people seven exist, even if one is not functioning now and may never function again.

The personnel of the larger cofradías consists of one alcalde who is its head and who formally receives the saint for a year; one mayordomo who serves as alternate head; six cofrades who carry on tasks under the direction of the mayordomo and the alcalde, three serving each alternate week. The smaller cofradías have only four cofrades in their organization.

The nominating committee is having trouble staffing these cofradías, and this accounts for the temporary nonoperation of the small cofradías of *San Pedro*. Part of the difficulty of finding individuals willing to serve comes from the fact that 161 Protestant families are withdrawn from service; part from the reluctance of factory personnel to serve; and part from the changing relation of the civil to the religious hierarchy and accompanying sanctions of authority. The mechanisms for compelling one to serve in the cofradía system are informal sanctions about discharging public duty and being a good citizen. The rewards of service are honor and prestige, and eventually a voice in village affairs when one has served in the top posts of either wing of the civil-religious hierarchy. Factory workers appear slightly more reluctant to undertake service in these cofradías than does the general population. During the last year, it is true, the cofradías were about 40 percent staffed by factory personnel, which is more than their proportion of the cofradía staff. However, I was told by the members of the Comité that it is generally more difficult to induce factory workers to undertake service than nonfactory workers, and that year may be exceptional. Judging from conversations with eligible factory works of young or middle age who have never served in the cofradía system, I believe this is true. And their reasons for not serving or for their reluctance to serve reflect some factory influence upon the disposition of their time.

There is some minor loss of time in the taking of cofradía service, particularly on the weekends, as well as some financial loss. Many workers responded to this by saying that they did not want to spend their "free" time in the cofradía or be bound to be present at the many ritual occasions where cofrades are required, or to march in the funerals when an elder dies, or to spend long hours in lighting candles to the cofradía saint and his counterpart image in the church. These workers preferred to serve the community only in the civil wing of the hierarchy, saying that they thus gave public service as well as if they served in the religious offices; furthermore, there were fewer offices to go through and one was done with community service much earlier.

These kinds of statements at least reflect the newer recreation

orientations of the factory workers, as well as their more frequent
trips to Quezaltenango on the weekends. More generally, they
reflect the declining instituational prestige of the cofradía system
in village affairs, brought about largely through the efforts of the
young union leaders. The reluctance of factory workers to serve
in the cofradía system must be only slightly more than that of
the nonfactory workers, or else I should think that the seventh
cofradía could easily be staffed. The conclusion is much more
tenable that the cofradía system is going through a cycle of strong
and weak support, which I understand from older informants has
been true of this system; it is now at one of its low points, and at
this point the factory worker supports them less than the nonfactory worker.

I say that the system is merely going through a cycle because
I find that factory workers and nonfactory workers still subscribe
to the value system of cofradía support, to cofradía importance,
and to the necessity for religious brotherhoods, and because of
the important role such a system plays in structuring the entire
society on a basis of age and prestige. It is the one mechanism,
in conjunction with the civil branch, which relates family to
family in an orderly manner and enables members of the community to relate to one another in the customary formal manner
without the necessity for extended personal interaction.

The worker believes that the community must be in harmony
with the saints and the special provinces of the supernatural
which they control, and that this harmony can be achieved through
care of the saints by the cofradías in the public name. Along
with the farmer, he feels that he is being represented when the
cofrades say their orations march in their processions, and carry
on their sacred roles. He would be just as uncomfortable as the
nonfactory worker if the cofradías did not exist. He shares approval and belief in the content of the cofradía symbol system—
its silver *escudos* of office, its litanies, its candle burning, its incense
offering, its *tambor* playing, and all its sacred paraphernalia
which he takes to be costumbre. And he reacts just as does the
nonfactory worker against the priest's efforts to purge the cofradías of some of their dramatic but unorthodox elements of
ritual and belief. In short, there is no divergence in emotional
attachment or intellectual subscription to Folk Catholicism on
the part of the workers. The divergence between practice and
belief seems to be slightly larger among factory workers, and

this appears to be related to the other possibilities for utilization of time open to them in a situation where the prestige of cofradías is at what I take to be one of its recurrent low ebbs.

In Esoteric Practices

The extent of the worker's adherence to the tenets of esoteric belief is not so easily discernible. The clients of the chimanes form no visible social group and hence show no social emergence where participation may be gauged. One proceeds here only by deducing belief from a knowledge of who uses chimanes. We knew of no adult in Cantel who was not aware of the existence of the sacred divinatory calendar or who did not know something of the meanings attached to the day gods in that calendar. Only the specialists know the ordering and numbering of the day gods, but everyone may be said to possess a fragment of such specialized knowledge. From talking to the nine operating chimanes in the municipio, I find that their custom is mixed as to worker and nonworker. There appears to be nothing in the occupational role of factory worker or in the experiences of factory work which would turn an industrial employee away from the use of esoteric specialists for the things in which they are considered expert. I have seen factory workers in consultation with chimanes in the same awefilled and respectful attitude as nonfactory workers, and women in the factory often come to the unofficial "alcalde," Manuel, to complain of being hexed, thus showing their belief in the chimanes' powers. There is a general sentiment that chimanes, through their use of esoteric knowledge and rite, communicate with spiritual forces that are sometimes extremely important to the welfare of an individual, and the factory workers subscribe to this. In fact, one of the practicing chimanes runs a machine in the spinning line in the factory. This industrial work has affected neither his practice nor his reputation, and he combines the newest and oldest elements of cultural content without conflict or seeming anomaly.

There appears to be a shift in the functions of the chimanes from curing to predicting: they have always done both, but now the divinatory aspects are clearly paramount. I cannot be sure, but this may be due in part to the fact of workers' medical services and the presence of a doctor on the factory grounds, and to the general preference for patent medicines and injections among the Indians of many rural areas.

In the Cult of Spiritualists

The cult of spiritualists was founded, and is headed, by a factory worker. But the 30 or 40 spiritualists who regularly attend his meetings are almost all farmers, with one or two Ladinoized non-indigenous Indians who are employed in the factory. The spiritualist cult is said by its adherents to be an extension of Catholicism and not in conflict with it. It has little general appeal to the Cantel Indian and is an imported phenomenon, very popular among the rural Ladinos of Guatemala. The situation of the spiritualist cult points up one aspect of the factory situation vis-à-vis religion or ideology. New elements in the life of the community are more likely to be imported by a factory worker than by a nonfactory worker. I suppose this is due to the factory worker's greater frequency of outside contact, seen in his more frequent visiting of the urban settlements of Quezaltenango and Guatemala City, and to his economic ability to buy more that he sees. These imported elements, as in the case of spiritualism or of political action, may not diffuse among either the workers or the rest of the population. What is important here is that workers provide a channel for the introduction of new elements into the larger population, and serve as the antennae of the local society in its contact with the Ladino world.

From this cursory description of the worker's religious life as compared with the nonworker's, the fact emerges that factory experience has not made a significant modification in the worker's adherence to and practice of the traditional religion, nor has factory experience resulted in a proliferation of cult and special creed among workers. They have used the content and symbolic system of traditional religion to give themselves a mystic identification which, I hypothesize, makes for a smoother and tighter integration of the factory settlement.

WORLD VIEW

I shall now briefly note some aspects of the world view of this community which workers share with nonworkers, and some minor divergences between these two categories. The world view of Cantel will not be described in detail; I shall limit myself to characterization of its prevailing axes, which is sufficient for the comparison. The world view of this community is structurally similar to that of other highland Indian communities (Tax 1941).

It is small—restricted in spatial range and in absolute content; it is animistic—parts of nature and the supernatural are thought to act and feel much like men; it is metaphorical—one part of the content comes to be associated with another by the process of linguistic extension rather than by logical nicety; it is local—only members of Cantel Indian society have it and share it. A further word on its content. Most of the elements which make up the Cantelenses' definition and apprehension of reality are historically derived from their Quiché ancestors and from the Spanish conquerors of the 16th century, worked over by time and local circumstance into their particular heritage. Few elements are of the modern or post-colonial world, which indicates another possible characteristic of the world view—it is a closed system, set in its ways and not easily absorbing new or foreign elements.

Major Tenets

Workers and nonworkers agree on the main tenets of the world view. Almost any member of the community can recount the Pueblo origin myth: that the Virgin Mary appeared three times on the present site of the church and each time was moved to a new place, always returning and telling the people to found Cantel here. Unlike our Santa Claus tale, it is believed to be an accurate description of why Cantel is where it is. The mythical names of the mountains and volcanoes that surround the municipio and the names of their owners, the spirits who inhabit them, are part and parcel of everyone's geographic knowledge. All know why four crosses mark the entrances and exits of the municipio—that with this symbol a *nawal* or guardian spirit keeps evil from entering the village. Common to all are the beliefs that the Sun, Moon, and Earth are deities in the kinship categories of father, grandmother, and mother. One can see, as I did, the dramatic acting out of these beliefs on the occasion of the moon's eclipse. When the moon is in eclipse it is a sign that the grandmother of all humanity is ill, and the people's hearts ache. Fires are lighted on the hilly periphery of the municipio to call back the "heart" of the moon, and all sorts of containers are beaten upon to drive the evil from the moon. People cannot look at the moon when it is in eclipse for that would make it ashamed, yet it is important not to let it out of their sight while it is ill, so they watch its reflection in pans of water set in their yards. All during the eclipse they solicitously watch the shadow move across the face of the moon. When the shadow passes, there is a collective sigh of relief as people say, "Now she has recovered." The drama of the eclipse involves the whole Pueblo. Fires are lighted on all the eminences nearby and noise emanates from almost every place. People are deeply concerned during the illness of the Moon Goddess because it means an imbalance in the relations between the people and the supernatural. The Moon is sick because of the sight of their sins. Activity during the eclipse assures the Moon, Sun, and Earth that the people still adore them and will revere and attend them as befits those dependent upon such strong forces for their continued existence. This explanation is available on inquiry from anybody in the village, factory worker or not. The municipio is one in this delicate and profound set of beliefs about the world. During the eclipse the noise and fires came from the factory settlement as well as from the nonfactory settlements. And all in Cantel share the meanings associated with the eclipse of the moon—if the whole moon is covered in an eclipse, the old will die in great numbers; if the shadowed part resembles a new moon, the young will die; and if the shadow covers only half, the middle-aged will die, for the forces of nature make retribution for the neglect shown them during the year. A pregnant mother must not see the moon in eclipse or have its light fall upon her lest she have a child that is mute or lame.

It is possible to go through item after item of the Cantelense world view and show the equality of belief by factory and non-factory worker. The unquestioning acceptance of the folk definition of reality is part of everyone's life, even those who are nominally converts to the Protestant creeds. Cases could be mustered to show that both workers and nonfactory employees believe, for example, that one can meet frightening spirits on the road and die of fright from this experience; that lightning is controlled by archangels; that to dream of an owl is a sign of death; that on *todos los Santos* one puts out food for the spirits of the dead; that the sacrifice of a sheep is necessary to keep death away from a new house; that the smoke from candles carries one's prayers to the gods; and a host of similar beliefs and practices. What I am attempting to establish here is the virtual coincidence in the view of the world held by Cantelenses, irrespective of their occupational roles. The listing could be extended to include the folk remedies, the modes of cure, the notions of hot and cold, familiar in broad outline to Mesoamerican experts, but I shall forego the additive value of these extensions.

No Transfer of Traditional Categories to Factory Experience

The coincidence of spheres of rationality and irrationality in the definition and manipulation of the world found to obtain between factory workers and nonfactory workers is the more striking since the factory worker is intimately connected with the sphere of rationality involved in the operation of the machinery which he tends. Two things may be said about the factory worker's regard for and apprehension of the technological complex of the mill: first, he has not animated the machines or the sources of their power, nor endowed them with demons or spirits; and second, the rational, albeit nontheoretical understanding, of the operation of machines and the sources of their power has not spread into other areas of his scheme of explanatory concepts. This bespeaks a compartmentalization in the world view of the factory worker. He does not extend the "principles" of customary explanation to his factory work, nor does he incorporate what he knows about factory operation into his customary principles.

I think the lack of extension of customary principles is easily accounted for. Working at the spinning and weaving machines, the factory employee carries on technical processes analogous to those carried on by the artisans who run the hand looms in Cantel and in nearby Indian villages. The loom, after all, is not an unfamiliar device in this section of the highlands. The repair and maintenance of factory looms is carried on by Cantelenses, who have learned the rudiments of mechanics and repair from the British engineer. He taught them without the use of either physical theory or animistic conceptions, and made of them craftsmen who can repair a machine without being fully aware of the principles by which it operates. A Cantelense factory worker is able to understand enough mechanics so that he needs no extra forces to explain how the machine works. Much the same can be said about the electricity which powers the machines. There is a turbine right off the main room of the factory which converts the water into generated power, and the Cantelense knows there is a connection between the operation of the turbines and diesels that eventuates in the "charge" that is the electricity which runs the machines, lights the lights, and plays the radios. More than this they do not know; I know little more myself about electricity, yet

like the Cantelense I find no need to erect intervening magical
or mystical concepts to cover the gap in knowledge.

In the factory, as I have pointed out earlier, the work routine
and the approach to the machines is in terms of the task to be
done—the production of cotton goods or thread and the smooth
running of the machinery. There is no ritual in approach to the
machine, in the operation of it, or in the explanation of its break-
down. No factory man thinks, if his production is low, that the
machine has an animus toward him; he will call one of the
mechanics to check or even, to the owners' distress, take a crack
at fixing it himself—but with screw-driver and pliers, not with
candle and copal. Should one care to elicit what the factory worker
knows about the operation of machines, he would get a picture
of a craftsman who understands only the cruder aspects of the
mechanical operations, much as I suspect one might find on an
American assembly line. But his approach and address to the
machines is the impersonal, unmythopoeic kind supposedly characteristic of machine line workers in an industrial society of
rational world view.

Factory Rationality Not Extended to Other Experience

The clear understanding, minimal as it may be, of the
mechanical operation in terms of physical causality does not lead
the worker to seek such cause and effect relations in other aspects
of his experience. This is more difficult to account for. It is socially
true, as pointed out, that workers make the same kind of metaphorical connections between many things as do nonworkers. For
example, the worker has not posed agricultural work in terms of
soils, seeds, fertilizer, and care. These rational aspects are included
by the better farmers. But both factory and farm workers consider
it of equal importance to offer thanks for a harvest in the form
of a *tioš jal*, a cross made of the largest ears set in the center of the
harvest and later on the house altar. Canteleños universally believe
this act is intimately connected with the outcome of the future
harvest and an instrumental part of the technology of maize farming. I have no reason to offer for this, except that such fundamental
antithesis between physical causality and mystical causality may
exist in the mind of an individual without causing psychic stress
or even an awareness of inconsistency, as it now does among the
factory workers of Cantel. A man's world view need not be of a
piece. Logical incompatibilities do not necessarily evoke psycho-

logical counterparts. It is with such aphorisms that I can speak of, but not account for, the apparent dichotomy in the world view of the factory worker.

There are, as will be pointed out in the section on the leaders of the union and the holders of new ideology, Cantel factory workers who are more sophisticated, whose world view more nearly approaches ours in scope and content. But this development may not be construed as the automatic extension of rational principles deduced from the exposure to and manipulation of a machine technology. For such spontaneous generation of ideas and thought systems does not arise from experience with machines, as the world view of most Cantel factory workers attests. Rather, we must conceive of technical experience as generating a set of problems, the solution of which depends upon refinement of propositions through the social processes of dissemination, acceptance, and integration into a prevailing thought system and within a given social structure. Perhaps because the Cantelenses see the institutional locus of understanding and rationalization of the continued operation of the factory as lying beyond their society and their immediate control, they have not felt pressures to assimilate the machine fully to their thinking. What would happen if the factory's operation depended strictly upon the local society is open to speculation. It is problematical whether such conditions would be the fruitful source of the generation of myth and ritual and magical practice to insure continued operation of the factory. Here I shall do no more than reiterate the fact that work at machines, the operation of which is conceived in rational causal terms, does not act as a solvent upon the extra-empirical thought system covering other aspects of the worker's life. Those who have changed the nature of their world view have done so through their attachment to institutional structures which have different world views, rather than through extension of such causal principles as they may have learned in the factory to other areas of their lives.

7
The Personality Component

MY UNDERSTANDING of Cantel personality depends entirely upon what I have learned through the normal processes of social interaction with many individuals, and the observation of them in various social situations during my stay. I gave no projective test or used other special techniques to get at the "deep" aspects of individual personality. I find this no great handicap since I shall be discussing what has been called the "public" personality as contrasted with the "private" personality (Lewis 1951). And I shall talk of the personality component of some Cantelenses from what has been called the "cultural deductive method" (Wallace 1952). To be fully explicit, I mean to recast in psychological terms, and to fit those terms to some individuals, part of the social and cultural behavior reported earlier. I shall be abstracting from responses made by individuals in social situations a person's ability to muster a certain psychological syndrome and "energy" in the performance of roles and social tasks.

There appears a wide range of personality type both among factory workers and nonfactory workers. No one category will hold the people of Cantel, and since I did not plan to study frequencies of postulated types, or of particular traits or items of personality, it is beyond my present power to state a determinate frequency. Individuals can be found in Cantel who are aggressive, placid, with strong egos, and with weak egos, whose behavior is controlled largely through guilt feelings, or whose personal control system rests upon shame and fear sentiments. There are persons who are quick of speech and movement and those slow of speech and movement, persons who are open and frank and those who are shy and timid, persons who are affable and gay and those who are suspicious and morose. There is a wide gamut of personality traits, but certain currents and certain traits are most commonly repeated in the personal makeup of Cantelenses. I cite those which are apparent in the social behavior or public performance of Cantelenses, and which by their frequency of occurrence distinguish the Cantelense, even for the casual observer, from the surrounding Ladinos and from a North American.

In normal social interaction such as a chance meeting on the street, in public gatherings while sober, when anyone not of the household may observe them, Cantelenses are reserved and undemonstrative. Their greetings to each other depend upon age, sex, status, and other structural criteria. In public the overtone of joy or sadness or surprise that a meeting might occasion is so suppressed that the observer can catch only the barest hint. This absence of emotional demonstrativeness is a quality which permeates all public or visible social relations. It is the result of great personal control mechanisms coupled with the desire to keep one's feelings private and to reveal them only under the proper circumstances. Reserve kept by strong internal controls may then be taken to be the first characteristic that a stranger would, if long enough resident, consider a part of the Cantelense social character.

This reserve often verges on what might be called placidity. People seldom show excitement unless drunk. In the face of minor catastrophe or personal hurt and injury a Cantelense may be expected to keep a calm exterior, whatever he may feel internally. In the instances when I have dressed the wounds of individuals badly cut by a machete, the wounded man sits calmly, never uttering sounds of pain or contorting his facial muscles to suppress the pain, while those around him view the wound with apparent lack of concern. This stoicism is highly valued. When a man reported the effects of a landslide which had killed thirteen people the night before, he did so in matter of fact tones, adding only the conventional "que lástima!" at the end of a gory recital which included the description of corpses gnawed by dogs and a mother and child struck dead by a falling boulder. His hearers received this news with the same apparent lack of strong emotional reaction, and a party of ten village officials who went later to make official witness of the event returned to reiterate with what impressed me as remarkable sang-froid the horrible details of the incident. This reserve and placidity in the face of strong stimuli gives the impression that the Indians are stolid and do not feel deeply. I think this is not true, given the great demonstrations of grief or joy that are expressed under the permissible conditions of funerals and weddings, usually under the influence of alcohol. What is involved in the normal pattern of social interaction is a positive personal effort to bleach out strong emotion; this results in a social character which in most situations is reserved, placid, nearly unemotional, and often stolid in the face of deprivation.

Coupled with this is the great patience Cantelenses are capable of exhibiting. They are able to keep in check any impatience at a long waiting period. Nothing should be desired in a hurry, nor is anything expected to be achieved easily and quickly. As they say, "paciencia quiere la vida" when the car which is to take them to the city is three hours late; when they come four mornings in a row to see the alcalde and wait hours on end without an interview; when they wait five years to get together the money to make a house sacrifice; when they save pennies and quarters over the years to buy another cuerda of land. In the thousand little delays and setbacks in daily life they wait without tension and without apparent bitterness. They are a patient people.

They are a cautious people; bold plan and execution, large design and great enterprise are alien to them. "Poco a poco," bit by bit, is how they like to see things done and how they like to do things. For example, a man does not conceive of repairing a house in its entirety, even if that be the need. He thinks of doing this now and then something else later. Even the richest man in the village puts up a new wall on his patio one year, a new door the next year, and plans to fix another part of the house the year to come. All new situations should be, and usually are, approached with caution. Do not leap into a purchase or a sale, into a promise or a debt, into a friendship or an enmity, the Cantelense will tell you. Anything done is sure to be greeted with approval if it can be said it was done "con cuidado," with care, a cautious wait until the whole situation was revealed before responding.

The repression of overt emotion, the traits of patience, caution, and placidity, are particularly marked in the women, who must restrain themselves not only in public but within the family. Women are not expected to cultivate the elementary social skills with which most men equip themselves to enter into public and religious life. They tend to define themselves only in their domestic responsibilities. Women speak of other women in two categories— the industrious who are well versed in their role of housekeeper, and tale bearers who linger to gossip in the streets or at the fountain. Women without formal social skills give the impression of immaturity. They are bashful and shy if attention is drawn to them in public, and this withdrawn behavior is encouraged by training. Women are instructed in modesty and told to run from men who attempt to speak to them, and are advised not to encourage friendships with unrelated women. They are an exaggerated version of men's public behavior, without the social skills to give as placid a front as men are able to muster.

These qualities of reserve, patience, and caution often make the Cantelenses seem, to Western eyes, slow-witted or dullards. But this is not so; they learn quickly, if the conditions are right as in the factory, and many are keen observers of their fellow men. It is only the necessity of exercising personal controls to appear reserved, calm, and prudent in public behavior which gives the social life of Cantel its characteristic tone of an unruffled, even tenor, of a placid, emotion-free existence.

Looked at another way, these characteristics of the Cantelenses bring to mind the adjective "tough." (A colleague says the adjective "dogged" comes to his mind.) They are tough in their ability to stand pain and shock, in their ability to bounce back from such injury and upset, tough in their lack of complaint, tough in their mode of attacking a large task bit by bit, and tough in the minimal nature of the comforts and blessings they expect from life. The Cantelenses are a tough and rugged people, and proud of these qualities.

Cantelenses are continually preoccupied with scandal and gossip. A neighbor's good or at least neutral opinion is sought after and highly valued. This opinion is gained by the proper conduct in public affairs and by avoidance of the sharp personal battle which nearly everyone in the municipio has had at some time. It is easy to alienate the good opinion of one's neighbors for some minor breach or some direct dispute. Cantelenses are given to gossip, mostly malicious, about one another. Everyone knows that he is being judged and talked about, and if he commits an egregious error or comes to public notice for some opprobrious reason, a Cantelense may sulk in his house for days or weeks, not walking the streets or seeing anyone because of his shame. The police commissioner, a good friend of mine, lost his job because he was drunk on duty one day. After the relief from his post he stayed in his house for more than two weeks, seeing no one but his immediate family. His wife also restricted her comings and goings. He knew of the hostility toward him—rooted, he said, in envy. His predecessor in office was a man of sterling character, but also lost his job on the charge of drunkenness. It is said that his enemies waited ten years before they found a pretext to have him fired. This envy and the gossip it brings in its train is said to come to those who become too prominent or powerful, or socially visible. The village secretary was also turned out of office by malicious gossip and a public demonstration which cast the blackest aspersions upon his character. Bootleggers are usually denounced to the public authorities by a Cantelense who is either full of envy or who has had a quarrel with the illegal maker of spirits. When I visited my friend the ex-commissioner in his home, he was worried about what others were saying of him and had exaggerated ideas of how much he was being maligned, but his state was a reflection of the social fact that malicious gossip follows upon small or large occasion for its unleashing.

From this flows, I suppose, the quality of suspiciousness that appears to permeate much of the personal interaction in Cantel. Cantelenses are not open and frank in conversing with each other, but neither are they devious or cunning. Rather, they are suspicious as to motives, reasons, and ends when one asks questions or seeks information. No one but a parent or sibling can be trusted with a confidence. They tend to give those answers which they think are called for rather than true answers, if the truth will make for hostility or discomfort. They suspect that what anyone claims to be about is indeed not the case. And they have grounds, since nobody ever really tells anyone else exactly what he is about, if that person does not have an imperative need to know. For example, the street greeting is often, "Where are you going?" to which the reply is, "I have my errand." This covers the general situation and gives the culturally expected and valued excuse of being busy. This suspiciousness often gives the Cantelense the appearance of being secretive, since revealing purpose or plan may lay one open to the interference of a hostile neighbor or jealous enemy.

With this suspicion and secretiveness always near the surface, Cantelenses are easily given to fears. They are not fear-ridden, for indeed they appear a cheerful, easy-laughing people with a fine sense of the ridiculous, and even responded to my brand of Spanish jesting. But fear can easily be injected into a Cantelense, and most untoward things raise large fears. If the fear cannot be easily contained, a Cantelense avails himself of the cultural mechanism for releasing his fright. He may get sick from *susto*—fright caused by such things as meeting a spirit on the road, or falling into a hole in the dark, or from any unexpected happening. When he gets susto he is literally ill, and people take care of him as if he had a physically caused sickness. Through this care and the social acceptance of his fright as a legitimate reaction, he is able to recover and bring himself back into psychic balance. Some Cantelenses have died from susto, revealing, I think, the extremities that fear may reach in their personalities.

Not only fear, but strong emotion is hard for a Cantelense to handle. People who continually show strong emotions have some sort of "bad blood" which they have inherited, or else they are said to be badly reared. For the ordinary person to have a strong emotion, be it joy or sadness, is to have an equally depressing reaction—given cultural names such as "dolor del corazón," pain in the heart; "mal del estómago," upset stomach, and many other ailments which habitually follow the indulgence of strong or unbridled emotional reaction.

When Cantelenses leave the even tenor of their ordinary social mood and give in to a strong emotion, they are completely dominated by it. When they grieve it is with loud wailing and anguished cries in an ambient of super-charge that usually lasts from four to seven days. If reminded while drunk of a dead parent, the tears will flow freely and the sadness is great, loud, and genuine. They are much more easily submerged in sadness than in gladness, and I have never seen nor heard of a Cantelense roaring with laughter. When they yield to anger, they are very angry. A man in a fight, which is rare, comes near hysteria in his anger, often crying and shouting and tumbling out words between sobs. An angry woman may shriek and sob and rant when given to her outburst. The bounce-back from strong emotion is often very rapid, and a sober man who was uncontrollably angry may an hour or two later appear entirely composed.

Upon this basis of suspicion, fear, gossip, and inability to handle strong emotion, rests the Cantelense's ability to be aroused easily into aggressive or hostile behavior. This aggression is never very far from the surface, and I know of only one man in the hundreds of inebriated Cantelenses I have seen who does not normally become aggressive when his control mechanism dissolves in alcohol. When drunk, men seek someone to brawl with, some object to pit themselves against, some wrong to redress, or commonly a domestic infraction which necessitates the beating of the wife. Women's aggression under alcohol usually takes the form of self-berating or of denouncing some neighbor. Channels for aggression are found in the gossip one can pick up, in such little acts as taking great delight in kicking a stray dog whenever the opportunity presents, in the frequent court cases over very trivial things, in the constant flood of accusation and denigration of coresidents. Cantelenses can be very petty and mean in the restricted outlets allowed to their aggressions.

With all this, Cantelenses are tolerant of a wide range of behavior so long as it does not impinge upon costumbre—certain manners, etiquette, and ritual behavior—which are the minimal musts to be a member of the society. Outside of this area of costumbre a man may do almost anything with no sanction other than gossip. For example, there are several cases of male bigamists known in the village, subject only to some minor gossip but treated on the streets with the deference and respect due them according to their public service and age. They will excuse foreigners' behavior on the grounds that everybody has his own costumbre, as they forgave my habit of entering a house without obeisance to the house altar until I learned that this was expected. With this tolerance is a lack of invidious comparison or covetousness. They are not unusually jealous of a man's possessions if he is liberal and charitable. There is the feeling of an even-handed justice in the partition of the world's rewards which is largely borne out by the social mobility and the change of economic status which takes place in the community. Sooner or later one gets his deserts, and there is no use fretting about an unknown future.

Cantelenses are not inventive, manipulative, problem-solving kinds of persons. They tend to take things as they find them, make them do, and use them in ways they have seen their fathers use them. They do not, for example, tend to innovate in furnishing their houses, rearing their children, or ordering their careers. They take what the world offers them without trying to seek a better way. I think of the Almolongeño who moved to Cantel and has a vegetable patch, the only one in Cantel. It does not occur to any Cantelense to start growing his own vegetables, even though this is demonstrably possible. The packets of seeds stocked by one store in the Pueblo only grow dustier and dustier. No Cantelense wants to innovate.

Yet, they are flexible in the face of innovations. The factory is now accepted as part of the natural landscape; the railroad that once whizzed by the Pueblo, the bulldozers that came to make the new national highway that is to pass below Cantel, the newly installed water system, and other such changes have their momentary upset in communal life and then are quickly taken as the "natural" part of the environment over which Cantelenses have no control. This can be put another way: as personalities, the run of Cantelenses have a streak of resignation to fate, be it of the natural world or of the larger social world, and when they see that a thing is inevitable they work out some kind of adjustment to it.

One final kind of personal trait strikes one about the Cantelenses. They are personally well disciplined and regular in habit. The clock is perfectly suited to the way they like to run their lives. An orderly, undeviating daily routine, seasonally adjusted, is an ideal nearly approached by Cantelenses. And this accords with the general lack of flamboyance or "style" in almost any aspect of personal life. There are no specialized skills in love-making, in cooking, in drawing embroidery designs, in songs, or in dances. Personal creative ability means a bread with tradition, and the Cantelense would be suspicious of it and perhaps would not even understand it. They have no desires or psychic energies to give to the creation of experience or beauty which passes ordinary and common occurrence.

The personality traits listed above do not exhaust what may be said about the Cantelense public character, nor do they provide enough data for the abstraction of a type capable of being stated with some economy. The usefulness of such a description of public personality lies, I think, in offering a portrait of the psychic energies and personal traits which characterize the people of Cantel. Such characterization is the more striking since it applies with equal force to the entire population; the workers are undifferentiated in their public behavior and thus in their public personality from those who have never submitted to the disciplined routine of centralized production at power-driven machines. This is perhaps a way of summarizing what I have said earlier about the cultural and social life of the factory worker as compared with that of the agriculturalist or artisan. The general point to be drawn from this observation is that factory work, in the conditions of Cantel, does not require, at least at the overt level, reorganization of a personality system developed in response to a significantly different occupational and work system. Some effect is visible among factory women, who, as a group, show a convergence in social ease to the male role, when compared to domestically occupied women. Viewed even more generally, one might infer that peasant and factory worker, as personalities, share enough common features to make the transition to another system of economic organization without basic modification in internal dynamics or psychic economy.

8

The Union: Extension of Social Horizons and Definition of New Roles

IN ADDITION to providing social situations which, to my eye, appear generative of personal and intimate relationships, the union involved most of the factory workers in activities remote both in concern and in kind of experience from the life of the *campesino*, while the sport teams and cycle clubs provided their participants with experience in organized adult play unassociated with ritual or rites of passage, a feature equally foreign to the traditional life of the community.

UNION MEMBERS ENTER INTO NEW
ORGANIZATIONAL ACTIVITIES

During our stay, scarcely a week went by without a meeting of the executive board or of the full membership of the union. Most of the factory workers attending these frequent meetings participated in a choice-making process, some features of which were absent from Cantel life, about issues often removed from immediate consequence and concern. The usual procedure at these meetings involved much discussion and finally a balloting on an issue about which members held differing opinions. Issues were generally raised by the executive committee of the union and then presented to the members. In the discussions there were two departures from customary Cantel life, while in the way a decision was reached there was near identity with the way groups in the community ordinarily arrive at consensus.

An example which illustrates both the workings of the union and the kinds of issues which were its concern is the instance of the proposed wage raise for employees of the factory who were "outside" workers—that is, they did not work in any of the manufacturing departments of the plant but were employed in ground maintenance and building care. These employees did not receive the minimum wage given to factory workers in the plant itself but they were members of the union and they had complained to the executive board of the union that their pay scale was inadequate. Would the union take it into consideration? The executive board held three closed meetings debating this question. From Juan M., then secretary-general of the union, I learned how the board decided to take up the cudgels in favor of the outside workers. The decision was made, Juan says, on the grounds that the union was obligated to resolve complaints of its members, and moreover the case provided an opportunity to test the union's strength and to prove both to the community and to the union itself that it was a power to be reckoned with. When the executive board agreed, the issue was presented to a full meeting. Juan made a speech in favor of presenting an either-or demand to the management of the factory—either a wage raise be granted, or there would be a general strike. Faced with a choice of accepting or rejecting support of the outside workers, the meeting gave way to a lively discussion. In the ensuing debate individuals rose to speak when recognized by the chair; there was no waiting for the older and more prestigeful persons to have their say first, which is the usual procedure in contested issues in Cantel. Both men and women rose to offer suggestions and explain their feelings. The exchange of opinion and feeling also departed from that exhibited, say, when the principales debated the water system, in that individuals actually made clear statements of opposition to each other. In group discussion in other circumstances, this is consciously avoided. If an individual holds an opposing view from another, he states his view as a kind of monologue, not taking up the argument of his opponent. And then he is done—without rebuttal, without defense of his idea, and without attempt at formal refutation of another's argument. The polite and proper way to go at a disputed issue in Cantel is a kind of democracy without debate, lacking modification of idea and position through communication. The union meeting was essentially different. Debate was against another's point of view and tried to show the weaknesses in someone else's argument, and the issue usually underwent some modification through the expression of different and opposed view-points in an atmosphere of spirited debate and argument.

These two differences in manner of discussion between union meetings and other assemblies were noted with approval by some of the more observant natives and decried by others. But whatever the cultural evaluation of them, as procedures for reaching group consensus they gave participants a training in manipulating opinion and in making personal weight felt which was far different from that of the average Cantelense.

However, the departure was not so great that a union meeting was a miniature replica of a town meeting in New England. The culmination of the choice process, expression by vote, was identical with the prefactory type and procedure. Argument and dispute continued until all had their say. In this case, three positions were taken. One held that the issue as presented by the executive board was worthy of support, come what may; another held that it should not be presented in either-or terms, that it was not worth going out on strike for 80 or so outside workers; the last position taken was that the wage increase was too much and that by asking for less, accord might be reached without strike or hard feelings on either side. These three positions came up with almost the first three speakers, but a vote was not taken until more than two hours of discussion had ensued. No vote was taken until it was entirely clear from the debate which issue was most popular and would win if a vote were taken. From the nodding of heads and the applause and murmuring after each speech and each rebuttal, it became clear that the position taken by the executive board had the majority of supporters. When this was clear to the assembly a vote was taken, not by count but by voice vote. Unanimity was registered. This is precisely what takes place in other choice-making situations in Cantel. For example, when the principales together with the municipal officers take an issue under consideration, each viewpoint is presented as a separate entity, not debatable or modifiable, with each man waiting his turn to speak in terms of age and prestige. But when one view is decided upon by general reactions of approval, it is always accorded complete unanimity. There are no minority positions registered, and no one wants to get on record as having had an opposed view. There is no righteous group of dissenters to say later, "I told you so." In the union process of arriving at a group decision, then, the procedures as to debate and public dissent followed a different set of norms from that apparent in other decision situations in the community, but the registering of consensus followed the accepted pattern of expressed unanimity without minority reservation.

I cannot say that all the members of the union subscribed to the techniques of making their individual opinion felt and winning converts to a viewpoint through democratic debate, essentially the liberal political viewpoint and method of opinion formation, nor can I say how many learned it. What can be said, I think, is that whoever learned these things learned them because of his occupational role and his ensuing membership in an organization connected with that role. Some union members and factory workers experienced and used ways of reaching group decisions that could be and, as will be pointed out later, were of importance in their institutional impact. At least, then, some workers were socially differentiated by the experience of political discussion undergone in the years of unionization. They had gained experience in the formation of a voluntary organization, the extension of loyalties on the basis of abstract ideals, the experience of personal intimacy on the axis of common interest, and the notion of manipulation of other parts of their social order as a result of the fact that they had successfully maneuvered the hitherto all-powerful textile management into a favorable settlement of conditions of work and wages. These experiences and understandings emerged as social facts in the attempted reforms and political activities discussed below.

UNION ACTIVITIES AFFECT SOCIAL INTERACTION

The friendship patterns and organized social play learned by workers on the job, in the union, and on sport teams served to give a different tone and quality to recreational gatherings of factory people as contrasted with agriculturalists. In the dances sponsored by the union, or where only factory workers were present, there was rarely a general drunkenness or a devolution into fisticuffs and brawls. At these dances a decorum was maintained, and a gayness without excessive use of alcohol. At dances or festal gatherings in the ordinary round of the community calendar—the fiesta titular, after Todos Santos, private affairs such as weddings, and the *entregada del nino*—there was, without exception, drunken behavior by almost all present, a high incidence of fighting, and much name calling and insulting talk. At the dances at which people paid to dance the formless native *son* to the tune of the marimba, that wooden xylophone-like instrument which means joy and abandon to the Cantelenses, most of the dancers were drunk to begin with and got more inebriated as time passed. These differences in group pattern were striking, and the more so since when workers mixed with agriculturalists on the traditional occasions of celebration they matched or equalled the drunken, brawling behavior of the adult Cantelense at play. My own opinion is that the situational

aspects of the recreation determine the response, and I am unsure
what role the factory experience itself plays in permitting this kind
of regulated recreation. I do not know if agriculturalists are able
to play in the manner workers do, supposing that they want to.
But only factory workers play in a form which is not the licensed
behavior of traditional recreation.

EXPERIENCES UNIQUE TO THE UNIONIZED FACTORY WORKER

I will mention now, without system or ability to evaluate their
meanings, some other experiences and activities which made the
worker socially distinct or possibly culturally different from the
nonfactory worker. Due to union connections and the union's link
with the national and international labor movement, workers were
called upon to take into consideration topics and issues far
removed from their daily concerns. Examples of these are such
questions as voting a token payment to another group of Guatemalan workers engaged in a strike which came up three or four
times in 1954, all voted on favorably; endorsing a national
government propaganda blast such as those against "Yanqui
Imperialismo" or those supporting the agrarian reform program;
marching in the May Day parade as an expression of proletarian
sentiment; sending a delegate to Vienna to represent Cantelenses
in a left-wing world trade union conference; the formation of a
political party; and discussion of the state of textile workers the
world over and in Latin America in particular.

These are concerns which only factory workers had. They are
activities in which only factory workers participated. Taken one
by one, they seem to be linked to no other action pattern, nor to
any set of attitudes or sentiments which characterize the factory
worker as against the nonfactory worker. Cumulatively, I suppose
a case can be made that these activities and experiences underlie
some of the personal differentiation between factory and nonfactory people. But from the way in which they were evaluated by
both factory and nonfactory persons, I am loath to give them
determinate roles in any social or psychological aspects of differentiation, except in one or two cases. It is true that these activities
served to mark off the worker from the nonworker, in the limited
sense of defining who carried them on and whose concern they
were. However, I think that this kind of marking off is not highly
significant socially. It entails, for example, no more differentiation

of the worker from the rest of society because he marches in a May Day parade, than does the school child's marching in the celebration of the October Revolution mark that child off from those who observed celebrations of earlier revolutions of a different character. I say this because Canteleños who march in the May Day parade do not know what the May Day observance means in historical terms, nor do they infer bonds of solidarity with other, non-Cantel workers who march with them in the parade. To most, the May Day doings are a way of showing support for the national government, which asks that they march. Support for the national government is forthcoming because Cantelenses are aware that the basis of their union, their high minimum wage standards, depend upon the national government. Similarly, giving funds to other workers or workers' associations is frequently justified in terms of support for a segment of the population which will in turn support the national government. The motive of worker solidarity or of class interest, of proletarian consciousness, is generally absent among union workers. Some of their leaders do have this orientation toward the larger society but their circumstances are special, as is their viewpoint. Again, sloganeering by the government against United States interests in Guatemala, particularly United Fruit land holdings and the large American Electric concern, does not enter into the mind of the Cantel worker as conscious dislike for "imperialism" or foreign exploitation. These concepts are foreign to the notions of the Cantel worker, as they are to the agriculturalist. The dissemination of slogans among the workers and the carrying of banners upon a government-sponsored occasion is, I suggest, tied through the same steps of reasoning from the pay on the job, through the union, to the government support of the labor movement, to the deduction of the worthiness of supporting the national government. Most Cantelenses have only the vaguest idea of what and where the United States is; imperialism is a concept their training and experience does not permit them to comprehend. The bounds of the meaningful world extend only as far as the capital city, and then not for all Cantelenses nor for all factory workers. I do not mean to suggest that the failure of these supralocal activities to bear fruit in Cantel is merely a matter of information and education; that were Cantel workers in less ignorance of the modern world they would develop or assimilate the notions of the antiforeign, nationalistic, lower middle class group which was then in control of the national govern-

ment. There are strong structural and situational blocks in the life of
the Indians of Cantel which prohibit the wide cultural dissemination
of such notions and the activities presumed to flow from them.

The Careers of Three Union Leaders

Anyone who did overcome these structural and situational
blocks to the incorporation of views of the modern world containing such elements as imperialism, nationalism, and exploitation
was indeed a factory worker. I can think of only three men who can
be said to have made such ideas part of themselves. These three—
the second secretary-general of the union, the delegate whom the
union sent to Vienna and later to Moscow, and a very active union
member—all had special experiences related to organizations and
power situations beyond the local boundaries of society. All three
have moved strongly in the direction of becoming "Ladinos," of
detaching themselves from the local society and its institutions,
and of becoming in style of life like the bearers of the national
Guatemalan cultural tradition, in its rural and lower class aspects.
I take this as presumptive evidence that such notions and the
activities connected with them are incompatible with the traditional life of Cantel. One cannot be an inward-facing member of
the Cantel *patria chica*, beset by its concerns, living within its rules,
carrying out one's social obligations and ritual duties in the social
organization, and yet deal with the complex aspects of the modern
world in political terms such as proletarian consciousness,
imperialism, and so forth. It is beyond one's personal psychic
economy, and it cuts one off from the activities and common ends
of the members of the small, conscious, and distinct local society.
It is too great a leap for an individual to make and still retain
sentimental attachment and social ties with the small society of
Cantel. And the life of most Cantelenses is such that these notions
have no meaning or bearing on existence or belief, so that they
cannot with ease become characteristic of any number of people,
even as cultural alternatives. Giving personal concern and allegiance
to such concepts as class solidarity, antimonopoly, exploitation
by foreigners, entails a turning away from the traditional axes of
Cantel life, the ultimate result of which is abandonment of the
local society and its culture.

These three men have in large measure done just that. It appears
profitable to explore their cases as clues to the sources of such
worker differentiation as might place a Cantelense in the factory-

workrolebeyondtheboundsofsocialusageandculturalunderstand-
ing both individually bearable and socially permissible in Cantel.

The second secretary-general of the union, one of those attracted
by the idea of an independent and sovereign Guatemala, freed
from foreign exploitation under the guidance of an aroused peasantry and working class, was one of the first factory workers to take
part in the formation of the union. As part of this activity he went
to the capital city and met with some of the younger leaders of the
national labor movement, especially the disgruntled ex-school
teacher, Victor Manuel Gutiérrez. The Cantelense was selected
by Gutiérrez as the special link between the Cantel factory and the
national labor movement. Furthermore, he was the special protégé
of the resident manager, who at that time was actively campaigning
to be nominated by one of the government parties for a seat in the
national congress. Thus from the near and far ends of his existence,
the secretary-general was promised a place of power both within
his local community and beyond it. He told me that at first he was
drawn by the respect and attention the labor leaders in the capital
showed to him and to the people he represented. He was also
pleased that the resident manager of the factory selected him as
the one to whom the union gains would be attributed. He rose in
the esteem of his fellow workers as a man who could successfully
deal with the plant management in its own terms. He frequently
visited the capital, on a motorcycle which he bought, taking Cantel's
problems for discussion and returning with ideas, plans, and
literature to read and distribute. He was put on a government
mailing list for book and propaganda distribution. He read and
thought about what the government was saying and doing because
he wanted to appear intelligent and win the respect of the Ladinos
he saw in the capital. For nine years he played the dual role of a
man of power in the union because he could deal with the management, and that of a man of wisdom because he could elicit the
support of the national government for the union, and he came to
take these ideas as personal goals even while his style of life changed
more and more to that of a Ladino. In keeping with his position
of liaison between Cantel and the national labor movement, he
became a believer and exponent of the ideas he transmitted. Part
of his power depended upon being privy to the national labor
leaders, and being privy depended upon being enough of a Ladino
so that communication and understanding could take place.

He was this far removed from Cantel life: he wore lemon-

colored gloves when he drove his motorcycle; the cut of his suit
was like a Western man's; he never wore a straw hat but only a felt
one; on occasion he appeared with a tie correctly tied against
a store-made shirt; his shod feet always had stockings; and he wore
eye-glasses. He had reached that degree of city dress which
announced to all that he was not completely of the world of Cantel,
for this costume indicates that a man has dealings outside of Cantel
with people who place a value on such things, unlike Cantelenses
who recognize in it only a symbol of the superordinate class. He
could talk of things, which he sometimes only half understood,
that other Cantelenses gave no thought to. His self-identification
as a member of the working class; the light of defiance in his eye
when he talked of an independent Guatemala; the sympathy he
could muster for persons in the abstract—the Asians, the colonials,
the American Negro, the unemployed—all show a widening of
mental horizon and an ideological commitment to things not of
the local community, the problems whose solution depended on
the will and might of people outside of Cantel. He also married a
Ladina and his children wore Ladino style clothing.

Physically, he had not moved from Cantel, although he did
that too when the national government fled before Castillo Armas
in July, 1954; but even then his life and meaning were not of
Cantel. He had become a marginal man in a society not yet ready to
tolerate much dancing on its periphery.

Another man, who later bore the stigmata of the local
Communist when the government which had given him honor and
place collapsed, reached for the modern world and away from
Cantel through the chance experience of representing Cantel on
the world stage. This man went as the local delegate to the World
Federation of Trade Unions conference held in 1954 in Vienna.
The union was asked to send a delegate and the choice fell on him
because the secretary-general, the man referred to above, was
cautioned not to go by the resident manager of the factory. The
delegate selected joined the other members of the Guatemalan
delegation in Guatemala City, and flew to Vienna via Brussels and
Paris. Two weeks of sitting in large meetings hearing the discussion of strange topics by delegates from many countries made little
impression upon him. He accepted the opportunity, offered by
the Russians, to visit a textile factory in Moscow. Dressed like all
the other visitors in a heavy black overcoat, high fur hat, a somber
black suit, shoes and tie to match—all provided by the Russians—

and accompanied by a Spanish-speaking Russian, he made a three-week tour of Moscow. He went to textile factories, to an opera, to the ballet, to museums—in short, he received the full-dress treatment. Later he visited workers' rest homes on the Black Sea, a whirl around the other side of the world, a place where his sister had said the sun had its home and resting place when night fell in Cantel.

When the delegate came home he read long reports he had been given at the meetings in Vienna, and talked of what he had seen in Moscow and in Europe. He was put in the position of having to defend the value of his trip to the local people who had financed him, and to appear knowledgable to those who questioned him in the capital on his return. Locally, his new knowledge and new connections were regarded with suspicion. He was under pressure to defend himself because the anti-Communist element of the society had accused him of going abroad "para vender la gente," to sell out his people to some foreign ideology and to make some strange tie with dark powers. He became regarded as a sort of alien, a resident stranger who talked of things abstract and possibly evil. He once was attacked on the streets in a brawl over his being a Communist.

This strain to justify and to rationalize and interpret his experience, both to himself and to others, started for him a process of concern with the modern world and its workings. He made frequent trips to the capital to talk to labor leaders there; he made friends with one of the Ladinos who was sympathetic to labor, although a clerk in the factory; he took correspondence courses; he read government literature on politics and economics; and he began to try to make himself a local político by taking active part in the formation of a party. I do not suggest that the experience of going abroad started this chain of activity. It did not. It served as the stimulus for this man's firm steps into extralocal society. His father was part Ladino, and he had learned much of Ladino culture and manner from him. He had married a Ladina, and in his home he lived much like a rural Ladino. But he lived within the understandings of Cantel and participated in the Indian society's view of the world, albeit with much variation from the way of the more orthodox monte Indian. It was the trip abroad, however, which gave him contact with conceptions outside of Cantel and with persons who shared these conceptions, and which allowed him to think concretely of relating himself to this other society. When the government fell in July, he left the village.

The third case was that of a factory worker born outside of Cantel but long resident in it and married to a Ladinoized Cantel Indian girl. This man was part of the original union organization effort and later became secretary-general of the local union. His efforts in the union, plus his ability to speak good Spanish and his wider experience, brought him into contact with representatives of the political parties then forming in Guatemala. He pushed hard within the union to make a formal alliance with the *Partido de la Revolución Guatemalteco* and often talked with members of that party in Quezaltenango and in the capital. He, too, read the government newspapers and propaganda releases and kept his ear to a recently acquired radio. As he saw it, he was bringing news of the outside world into Cantel and interpreting it. Through the union he kept disseminating information about events and issues far removed from the understanding and concern of the average Cantelense. He carried out this activity for nearly eight years and began to see himself as a political organizer, for in 1949 the union affiliated more or less officially with the PRG; in return, the village was given a new elementary school building. He saw himself as a guide and formulator of public opinion on things of which people would not even be aware were it not for his missionary efforts. From this kind of activity was forged his self-image as a local representative of the democracy and the October Revolution; local people considered him to be either a little weird because he always talked of things remote, or else specially informed because he could be depended upon to clarify rumors, bring information, and make strange things intelligible. He was to national information and world event what the female gossips at the pila were to local event and rumor—an initiator, systematizer, and disseminator. And he was regarded with the same mixture of wonder and fear and dislike because he was in control of knowledge not open to all but of import in their lives.

When the Arbenz government fell, this man was immediately accused of being a Communist and hauled off to jail. After three weeks he was cleared by the authorities and returned to the village. He did not return to factory work but opened a small shop in his mother-in-law's building and was hoping to set up a corn mill powered by gasoline motor. But the amount of social isolation he encountered, in the way people gossiped about him and in avoidance by former acquaintances, and the hostile attitude of the new alcalde, moved him to leave the village. When I left Cantel, he had made plans to take up residence in another municipio—to start over, still an apostle of the principles of the Arbenz government but biding his time until opportunity presented itself. He was beyond the horizons of any local society by reason of attachment to the ideology of a sovereign, economically strong Guatemala.

The three cases indicate the extremes of one kind of differentiation from agriculturalists and artisans. Some of the reasons why it did not become more widespread among factory employees are apparent in the necessary social and cultural cohesion of the small society which militate against such detachment. I believe these cases indicate that the self-reference of behavior to a group or ideology of wider scope than the municipio world makes one alien to it. And one can remain a member of the local society only insofar as that entity moves in the same direction as the deviant.

Many workers show similar, though less pronounced, degrees of differentiation along the lines of these three men at the extremes. It can be stated categorically that those who did become concerned with the larger world were workers, not farmers or artisans, and that they were all men. But of the more than 600 male factory workers, only thirty had to any extent identified with the outside world and the political revolution. These thirty were not removed from local life, but felt themselves so close to it that they quit the factory after the July revolution. Judging from two or three that I talked to, the motive in quitting was to remove themselves from an occupational environment which allowed them the possibility of becoming different from their neighbors. They wanted to put behind them all reminders of connection with a society that was not Cantel. As I was told by Benito, who had quit the factory and taken the job of priest's assistant, "Quiero ganar mi vida sin mezclarme en cosas ajenas"—"I want to earn my livelihood without mixing into foreign things."

The intention in exploring the above cases is to show what differentiation may take place for a few, and why it did not take place for the many. It is also intended to indicate the potential sources of institutional change within the community, and to illuminate how the national society may come to make itself meaningfully felt within the small worlds that make up Guatemalan Indian society.

9

The Institutional Setting and Its Adjustment to Factory Production

THE comparison of the factory worker and the nonfactory worker has established the kind and degree of social and cultural differentiation between them because of their differing occupational roles. The change is small and the differentiation such that a factory worker, with the exception of the revolutionary labor union leaders noted above, is not separated in life style, social behavior, or personality from the nonfactory worker. Such lack of obtrusive change permits the continued integration of the factory worker into his community. But the rate and kind of individual differentiation is not commensurate with the nature and degree of institutional change. The small changes or shifts in personal behavior may, over time, have a massive effect. They change the texture of the social fabric. The inadvertent consequences of individual behavior may result in the processes of social conduction and convection (Firth 1953:86).

It is this aspect of the accommodation of Cantel to the factory system that I shall now describe. Part of the description of the institutional structure has already been introduced in the comparison of the social and cultural life of the factory worker with that of the nonfactory worker. I shall recapitulate this with a different emphasis.

The institutions of the municipio of Cantel are of a piece. That is to say, there are no cultural norms in determinate social groupings which characterize one segment of the population as distinct from another. One cultural pattern and one social structure embraces the entire community of some 8,000. It is true that in the remote settlements, the separate homesteads around the peripheries of the municipal boundaries (monte), one may find the more *antigua costumbre* in some elements of behavior and belief. These features are present to a much lesser extent in the more densely settled semi-urban town, but the lag is not now so great that the monte dweller exhibits an institutional structure different from the town dweller, or that town and country are in any sense opposed.

If we make the assumption that the cultural pattern, defined as the range of socially standardized behavior, and the social structure are of a single cloth, then the question is whether this is of long standing and whether its content and the internal relationship of parts have become much changed over the period of factory operation. The problem has an historical dimension.

The reconstruction of local history in Cantel is hazardous. No documents of great importance for the small society are usable, and any attempt to pinpoint the wider trends of Guatemalan history to Cantel is not especially profitable at this level of problem (i.e., use of the conventional periods and kinds of Indians as defined by LaFarge [1940] or later amplified by Goubaud [1952] does not cast any light on local developments except at a remove which bleaches all individuality from Cantel). One must rely on a few faded maps, some loosely compiled population numbers, and the selective memories of older informants. These, together with the judicious use of the standard inference of turning space into time, permit one to sketch the contours of Cantel society of seventy years ago. There is also some reliance upon the work of previous ethnographers on societies of the same kind in Highland Guatemala.

It is difficult to see clearly the subcultural background to the coming of the factory. According to the earlier census of Cantel (Quarto Censo, 1924) and the later census in 1950, the population has been increasing rather slowly, gaining only some 2,000 since 1893. The accuracy of the figures is open to grave doubt, but a slow and steady population increase may reasonably be inferred from the new housing being built and from the nearly full occupation of present housing facilities. Cantel has more or less held its relative place in the rank order of populated places in the highlands over the past 60 or so years, which indicates again that no great population burst ensued from the introduction of the factory.

The factory has radically changed the settlement pattern of Cantel, even while the shape of the municipio itself has undergone great changes from other causes. If an old, prefactory map of the municipio (Figure 11) is compared to the maps made during my stay (Figure 2 and Figure 4), the extent of the change is graphically revealed. This has been dealt with in the section on settlement types.

ECONOMIC INSTITUTIONS

The economic institutions of this society are little changed from seventy years ago. From the time that the oldest informants can recall, the community has been based upon small, freeholding farmers growing milpa and wheat, with communal lands comprising nearly 15 percent of the total municipal area. The largest land holders have never been very large; except for an old estate held by the Urbina family which was broken into parcels in 1870, some 500 cuerdas have been the outer limit of wealth in land. Landholdings changed from generation to generation; large landholders never grew to be great ones, nor crystallized into a class of rentiers.

The agricultural technology of Cantel is much like it was seventy and more years ago—the pre-Columbian kit modified by the introduction of metal tools and beasts of burden, and the introduction of wheat into the Highlands in the 17th century. In this small landholding economy, wage work and hire were charac-

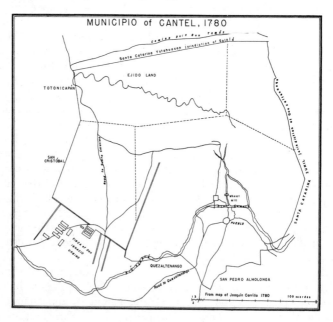

FIG. 11. Municipio of Cantel, 1780.

teristic. Cooperative or exchange labor was minimal. The primary producer marketed his own harvest, either in the local plaza or in the nearby corn-poor communities of Zunil and Almolonga. Wheat yields were marketed in Quezaltenango. Credit for farmers was not institutionalized. To raise money for production or consumption, land was pawned or sold. This kind of economic organization of farm production still persists in Cantel.

Special Occupations

Aside from the farm, other ways of making a living in Cantel were artisan or other special occupations—carpenter, mason, weaver, woodchopper, musician, barber, midwife, hatmaker, shoemaker, or tailor, traveling salesman, storekeeper, chimán, baker, tortilla maker, bonesetter, butcher, rain-cape maker, candle-maker, soapmaker or servant. No one made a living from the interest on loans or investments, or from manipulations of such small amounts of capital as then existed. These occupations, some of them not full time, are still on the roster. In addition to the jobs connected with the factory, there have been added the occupations of driver, miller, minister, assistant to the priest, paid police chief, paid alcalde, paid scribe, firecracker maker, clock repairer, milker, and teacher. Special occupations take up little of the work force.

The factory is not directly connected with the advent of the new occupations listed above, although many of them are related to the arrival of Ladinos or foreign Indians in Cantel. However, the factory has changed some of the disposal of work time for all Cantelenses. Thread and cloth were woven in Cantel and in surrounding municipios until about 1910. Women formerly had the task of spinning the thread with a wooden hand whorl, while both men and women used the backstrap loom and the small frame loom for making cloth that went into shirts, trousers, napkins, huipiles, and utility cloths. Today this domestic occupation of spinning thread is entirely absent, the backstrap loom is gone, and the small frame loom is utilized by about three men who make colorful cloth. The foot-pedal loom is still employed by weavers who make shirt material and shawls, but this art, as has always been the case, is learned in an apprentice relationship in Salcajá, San Cristóbal, or Quezaltenango, or from resident Ladinos or Ladinoized Indians. The use of factory cloth—unbleached muslin has the generic name of *Cantel* in the highland area—has made the spinning of thread and the weaving of cloth arts no longer practiced in Cantel. Their demise coincides with the factory's full production and resultant competition with the handicrafts, which seems to bear out the general observation that handicrafts disappear or shrivel in the face of factory textiles. The cheapness and durability of factory-made cloth are preferred over the hard and lengthy process of making inferior homespun goods, even if women's time were not economically significant.

The employment of nearly a fourth of the working population of Cantel has not significantly affected the labor supply for farm work, due largely to the former amount of "under-employment" on farm lands. Most families have more manpower than land at their disposal, and this results in such uses of time as a man and his two sons working 10 cuerdas, which is a job that can easily be done by one man. Another reason is that much of the factory work force is composed of women and young persons, who would not normally be income earners or employed in the business of farming. There is still more manpower available than tasks to be done in Cantel. People continually seek work at the factory, and no one ever complains of a shortage of laborers at harvest or planting time if he is ready to pay the going rate of hire.

Market Operations

The products of Cantel still are sold in the Sunday market, and the producers from the highland area—clothmakers from San Cristóbal and Salcajá, potters and woodworkers from Totonicapán, vegetable and onion growers from Zunil, Almolonga and Solalá, potato growers and metate makers from Nahuala and Santa Caterina, woollen goods and blanket weavers from Momostenango and San Francisco, and merchants of line, comales, copal, ropes, net bags, bananas, tropical fruits, eggs, store goods, silver work, and sandals—still bring their own products or carry those from the coast and city to Cantel. The transactions take place on a strictly cash basis in the kind of free market situation common in the highlands (Tax 1953). The factory has apparently had no effect on the Sunday market procedure, nor has loss of the community's minor handicrafts changed its importance or position in the rotating market system (McBryde 1945). The provision of commodities takes place today just as it did as far back as the longest memory reaches—through impersonal cash exchange in a fixed market place, with Cantelenses selling farm products.

There is more money in Cantel than there used to be, due to the cash wage of factory workers, and the Sunday market has spilled over into a smaller extension which meets in the factory area on Monday mornings. This market is a much reduced version of the Sunday plaza, but this second opportunity to buy things would not have come into being without the factory settlement and the cash paid to workers. Few Cantelenses come to sell in this market. It is made up of merchants traveling from the coast who stop over at Cantel, knowing that something can be sold to the workers even if it is not market day.

Supplementary to the Sunday plaza and Monday selling are the small shops of the municipio. These are merely the fronts of private houses rigged with a wooden counter, some shelves, a naked light bulb, a metal scale, and a glass case perched on one end of the counter. The stocks are small, the supply irregular, and the haggling of the open market place absent. Shops are old in Cantel. The first was owned by a Ladino around 1880, when there were only two shops in the municipio. Shops are still mainly owned by Ladinos, but two Indians have opened stores. There are nine liquor stores, which carry food and other items for sale. Although there are more stores than when the factory came, they still play the same secondary role in the distribution of goods that they did earlier. The only exception is the factory settlement store which stocks a range of goods including such items as ices for the children, cloth for suits and pants, canned foods, metal basins, commercial soaps, commercial candy, film, writing paper, school books, pencils, and pens. This store is a direct outgrowth of the presence of the factory, for the items it sells are not usually in enough demand in highland Indian towns to merit a stock in a local store. In other Indian communities, they are purchased from the traveling pitchmen in the plaza or on the Indian's visit to the city or Ladino center of a big town.

These changes have not amounted to remaking the economic structure of Cantel. The factory is superimposed on this peasant economy, drawing on the peasants for labor and returning cash, but the factory underlies the union's formation of new economic groupings and new economic values in the changed incidence of consumption items.

THE FAMILY

The family in Cantel, old informants say, is much like it was prior to the advent of the factory. By the mechanisms described in the workers' family adjustment to wage control and expenditures, one can see how this continuity has been maintained. The Cantel model is still the male-dominated bilateral nuclear family in a set of weakly defined extrafamilial relationships, with patrilocal residence followed by neolocal as soon as economic conditions permit. As indicated earlier, the worker may have a more integrated family life and reach the Cantel ideal with greater frequency than does the nonworker. Increased harmony with the ideal because of the greater wealth of the population is one of the changes at the institutional level. At the same time, people tell me that there is now much less respect for fathers and mothers, for older brothers, and for elders in general, than there used to be. I do not know if this is true, or if three generations ago I could have heard the same complaint. The people of the monte do in fact exhibit greater deference toward persons of respect within and beyond the family than do the people of the town or the factory settlement. The gestures of children waiting to be touched on the head before leaving the presence of an adult; the removal of the hat when greeting olders; the use of the *činla tat* or *nan* greeting for those of more age and prestige; the slight bow when meeting; the obviously greater command of a man within his home, all these things are more common in the rural settlements, and therefore serve to reinforce the people's contention that many aspects of the ideal family image, particulary the teaching of respect and manners, is more closely approximated in the monte. But I take this truth to be a relative one. That is, the *gente del monte* are changing in the same way as are the town and factory people but at a slower rate, and thus represent the outer bounds of the institutional structure rather than a fission in the cultural pattern. Fifty years ago, I am told, all the people in the town used the činla tat greeting, while those in the monte used a longer, more elaborate, and much more respectful greeting now found only in the semiritual salutations exchanged when *tartuleros* greet the kindreds at an old-style marriage ceremony. Other such items could be mustered to indicate the ripple nature of social change in Cantel—the original splash coming from the town, and now from both the town and factory settlement, with the waves moving toward the physical boundaries of the municipio. The point of this digression is that the Cantel family structure has made an adjustment to the factory without large internal modifications,

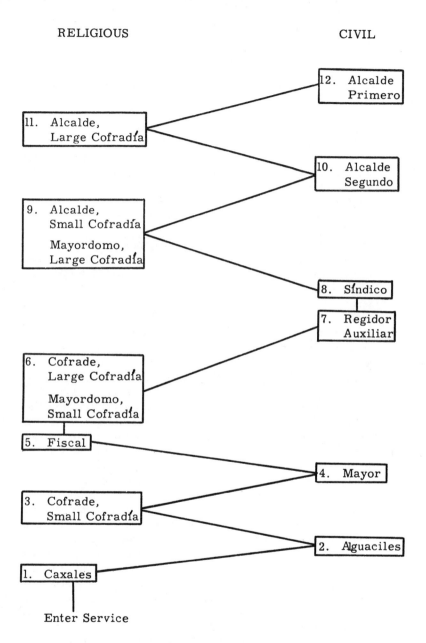

RELIGIOUS   CIVIL

12. Alcalde Primero

11. Alcalde, Large Cofradía

10. Alcalde Segundo

9. Alcalde, Small Cofradía

Mayordomo, Large Cofradía

8. Síndico

7. Regidor Auxiliar

6. Cofrade, Large Cofradía

Mayordomo, Small Cofradía

5. Fiscal

4. Mayor

3. Cofrade, Small Cofradía

2. Alguaciles

1. Caxales

Enter Service

FIG. 12. The former civil-religious hierarchy.

and that the family still articulates with the production system, the prestige system, the religious system, and the mode of social control as it did prior to the coming of the factory and wage work.

CIVIL-RELIGIOUS HIERARCHY

Apart from the family and the economic organization, the social structure of Cantel did experience change under the indirect impact of the factory. The basis of the social structure is the hierarchical system of civil and religious posts, which regulate the public life, dispense justice, and formally relate the community to the supernatural. This civil-religious hierarchy is the mechanism by which all families, through their male members, are interrelated in terms of prestige and public service.

All males were expected to serve, and most did. Seventy years ago the normal course of an individual in public life followed the path illustrated in Figure 12. A man became eligible for service some time between the ages of 15 and 17, and usually began to serve in one of the posts at about that time. The first post in the ideal progression was *caxal*, of which there were four, who worked as assistant to the fiscal. After a year as caxal, a man went to the post of *alguacil*, general messengers and cleaners of the streets and the plaza, following the three-year rest period which was characteristic between assuming posts. There were from 12 to 15 alguaciles at any one time. The posts of alguacil and caxal are fairly close together in rank and a man might begin in either post, although older informants say that being an alguacil was slightly above being a caxal. After an interval of three to four years in the alguacil post and the rest period, a man was eligible to serve as a cofrade in one of the smaller cofradías. From that post upward through the hierarchy, only married men were supposed to serve, since the duties of these offices required a wife; from this point in the ladder of office it is families, through their male heads, which are being used as the basis of selection. There were 16 men in the posts of cofrade of small brotherhoods in any given year. Following the post of cofrade a man advanced to that of *mayor*, the local policeman; there were two shifts of 10 men each week in this duty. From mayor the next post was that of *fiscal*, assistant to the priest and custodian of the church and its contents. There were two fiscales. Almost of the same rank, but always placed higher, is the post of cofrade of a large cofradía or *mayordomo* of a small one. The mayordomo is second in command of the religious brotherhood and in charge of the cofradías on alternate weeks. There were 12 jobs to be filled as cofrade in the large cofradías, and four mayordomos, making a total of 16 posts available on this rung of the ladder of office. The cofrades in each cofradía were ranked from 1 to 4, but this was used only as an adjustment to the differing ages in the appointments to that post; the older men serving as cofrades got the higher numbered rank, thus giving them superordination within the cofradía. To the outside observer, cofrades were ranked equally with civil office holders in terms of service to the Pueblo. A man next assumed the post of *regidor*, which is similar to our city councilman, or he could ascend to the post of *auxiliar*, a man who serves as the alcalde's representative in each of the seven rural cantones; since there were four regidores, there was a total of 11 posts at this level of advancement. The next post was either that of *síndico*, the keeper of the municipal records and exchequer, or alcalde of a small cofradía (4 posts) or mayordomo (3 posts) of a large one; at this point in the family's ascension in public office, there were eight posts to be filled. A man next became either alcalde segundo, the assistant mayor of the municipio, or alcalde of a large cofradía, the head of one of the three most important religious brotherhoods, making four posts to be filled at this level. From here he was eligible in terms of previous service and age to serve as alcalde primero, the mayor of the community who also acted as justice of the peace, performing marriages and sentencing minor offenders.

This is the ideal and often approximated picture of how a man served his community seventy years ago and before. From young adulthood until old age, he and his family were involved in moving between religious and civil office in public service. If a man started his service at 17 or 18, he would be at least 65 by the time he completed the ladder of offices and was at last free from public service. From the point of view of the individual the offices were considered a bother, since by serving a man and his family lost income and time. The discharge of an office used from one month to a full year's working time, and the offices were all unpaid in those days. Furthermore, the assumption of most offices involved the expenditure of personal funds at a ritual reception which, in the case of the alcalde of a large cofradía, sometimes cost as much as Q200. Men often delayed assuming the office when eligible, and sometimes cast about for acceptable reasons for postponing their turn or for extending the rest period between offices.

Functions of the Hierarchy

From the public point of view, the hierarchy entailed the manifest functions of caring for the administrative order of the community, providing police protection, dispensing justice, caring for the church, housing the saints, discharging the community's responsibilities to the supernatural by seeing that important feast days were celebrated by a duly constituted organization, and providing the body of elders who were the actual government of the Pueblo. Many men retired after holding post number 9 or 10 in Figure 12, but if a man passed through offices 9 to 12 he was considered a principal, and elder of the village entitled to deference and public respect and consulted in all matters of community interest. Decisions requiring the use of communal funds or manpower were always adjudicated by a joint meeting of the municipal corporation, that is, the síndico, the regidores, and the two alcaldes (who are all necessary at law to make a binding commitment for the municipio), and those principales who wanted to attend and offer their opinions. Nothing could be decided finally without the approval and public sanction of the principales.

The hierarchy is the link between the local community and the nation, on the one hand, and between a local world view and the Catholic Church, on the other. The requests and demands of the Guatemalan national government are transmitted to local Indian societies through officials of the hierarchy. Frequently, the functions of the hierarchy as an organizer of local society are not compatible with its role as the local extension of the nation (Nash 1956b).

The normal operation of the civil-religious hierarchy had the latent function of age-grading families, since the older families were higher on the scale and the younger ones were lower, and at the same time ordering them in terms of prestige, for the main component of social honor came from serving in the hierarchy; families and persons were placed in respect relations to each other from the discharge of public service. Thus, the system of offices carried on the public and spiritual business of the community and ranked its members in terms of social honor and graded them in terms of age. In the old days everyone knew who had served in what office, and thus what respect was due him and his family, almost by virtue of the age which the man had reached.

Cantelenses thought of the hierarchy as one system of offices, and in large part it was one system. The personnel was the same for both religious and civil offices, and no distinction was made between service in either set of offices or in terms of the discharge of public duty. Furthermore, the two sets of offices were linked by symbolic coincidences and reinforcing sanctions. From their knowledge of their neighbors, the principales drew up lists of those who were to serve in any given office. The alcalde of the municipio, using the sanction of the law, sent out an order to the persons named that their turn for office had come. The officers of the two wings were present at each other's installation ceremonies. When the cofrades took office, the alcalde and the rest of the municipal corporation came to the ceremony; when the alcalde moved into the juzgado, all the heads of the cofradías came to see him sworn in. Moreover, some of the nominally religious offices had secular duties, and the secular offices had religious duties. The cofradía of San Buenaventura, for example, was charged with burying the dead, including the opening of graves and the carrying of bodies to the cemetery. The municipal alcalde had the job of caring for the image of San Pedro, which went along with the office of alcalde and was considered the patron saint of the mayores and the municipal corporation. The unity of the two wings was thus a living reality due to the same personnel, the reinforcing sanctions, the symbolic linkage, and the mixture of sacred and secular duties.

Accommodations with the Factory

This system functioned in peaceful coexistence with the factory for more than two generations. The factory and the civil-religious hierarchy underwent minor mutual accommodations which enabled them to function in the same community. The public service histories of the older factory workers show the same progression from mayor to regidor and on up the ladder as do the histories of the older farmers. And until recently, factory workers carried on their public duties in both wings of the hierarchy.

The integration of the factory into the system of service was effected by simple modifications: when a man's turn came for office in the hierarchy, the factory would give him time off. In the case of mayores or guardias, who work one week on and one week off, the factory exempted them from work on their duty week and allowed them to work during alternate weeks. When one of their employees was elected alcalde, a two-year full-time job, the factory agreed to rehire him at the end of his service without loss of tenure. In short, the factory modified its work rhythm to allow its employees to serve in the hierarchy. Also, its work schedule granted holidays during Easter Week and the fiesta titular, the two most important holidays of the year, and it allowed for overtime so that there would be no great loss of income during these extended holidays.

When the factory had a problem relating to the community at large, the managers always called in the top men of the civil hierarchy for discussion. The managers often complained of the time these meetings took, but they never tried to by-pass the public representatives of the community. In some community projects, such as building a bridge over the river between the factory and the village, laying the floor in the local church, and building a road, the factory and the community were joint participants and financiers.

On its side, the community made some concessions to the factory. (For example, on Monday morning when the local jail was often crowded with drunks, the community would allow the removal of men necessary to run the machines, as described earlier.) The community did not try to run the factory and the factory did not try to run the village, after the initial period of adjustment described in the early history of the factory.

Effects of the Revolution, the Union and Its Political Parties

Until the revolution of 1944, the civil-religious hierarchy operated in substantially the manner described above. The slight shocks it had received from Protestantism, the depression of the 1930's, and the intendente system did not change its nature or deprive it of its functions (Nash 1955a). But with the advent of the revolution, a union was formed in Cantel which included the bulk of factory workers in the community. In its earlier aspects, the 1944 revolution was democratic in orientation and program and solicitous of bringing the Indian component of Guatemala into the national life in a meaningful social and cultural manner (Goubaud 1952).

The *Sindicato Trabajadores Fábrica de Cantel* (STFC) was an offspring of the revolution which legalized unions. The union was associated with the national federation of unions, which in turn was an important prop in the Arbenz government. Union leaders were in a position to receive first-hand the ideas of political democracy upon which the revolution was launched, and given the network of connections with the national government, they were assured that any attempts they made to implement these ideas and to organize political supporters for the national regime would be given full legal support by the agencies of the national government.

The revolution of 1944 promised free and open elections with full male suffrage and extension of the ballot to literate women, and it encouraged the formation of political parties. In the first flush of enthusiasm which swept the nation at the fall of Ubico and the election of Arévalo, only one political party, the party of the victorious junta of 1944, put up a candidate in Cantel. This man was elected alcalde without opposition, but he was eligible both by age and previous service in the hierarchy to fill the post. He was a factory worker but he followed the traditions of Cantel civil government. He consulted with the principales; he attended the cofradía openings; he took over the saint that went with the office he held; he nominated persons to fill other roles in the hierarchy at the suggestion of the elders; in brief, he was a typical alcalde, violating neither the principles of selection for office nor the rules of conduct.

But as the union gained strength and membership in Cantel between 1944 and 1946, the political ambitions of its leaders were aroused. Through the young men who had associated themselves with the ideology and program of the national government, the union was moved toward formation of a political party. The break with the official party, then the PAR, came about through a series of small events in local jockeying for power. A branch of the *Unión Campesina*, the peasants' organization sponsored by the revolutionary government, had come into being in Cantel. This organization was used by one of the campesinos to back him for the office of alcalde, which at this time paid a salary of Q60 monthly, one of the highest salaries in the community. At the same time, an anti-Communist party was launched in Cantel, the *Partido Independiente Anti-communista del Occidente* (PIACO), with a leader who also aspired to be the next alcalde of the municipio. The existence of these two organizations was construed by the leaders of the STFC as a threat to national government policy favoring unions and as possibly predisposing the municipal corporation in favor of farmers rather than factory employees in the distribution of local justice. The union also thought that it should make itself felt in local affairs.

In arranging for a unified government ballot for the 1946 elections, there was a dispute between the union men and the elders who were willing to be part of PAR, the government. This coincided with the national emergence of another prorevolution party, the PRG. The union leaders felt that the proposed candidates for the six top offices—alcalde, síndico, and the four regidores—which were nominally open to election, and which were in fact elected without opposition, were not those most favorable to the union, to the abstract ideals of the revolution, and to local progress and community welfare as they conceived it. At this time the union was in favor of bringing piped water to the village, and getting a national government promise to build a modern rural school for Cantel. The rest of the village was neutral toward this program, although the water system had been considered before and had often been debated without reaching consensus on a place from which to bring the water. The PAR put up its slate of candidates, with the union men feeling antagonistic toward it. The three men earlier called the ideological deviants, together with a retired school teacher, the Ladino telegraph operator, and a few others in the factory, decided to form a local PRG which would be responsive to the factory workers' needs.

This local branch of the PRG was formed, and for the first time in recent Cantel history, political parties in contested elections became a meaningful issue for the general population. The PRG put forth its own slate of candidates for the six top offices, but they were men not eligible by age or previous service to fill the upper posts of the civil hierarchy. They were young men, in their late twenties or early thirties, who had as a rule served only in one of the civil offices such as mayor, and some of them as cofrades. The election was carried out in terms of the ideal pattern set by Guatemalan law—secret votes at tables where representatives of the several parties were present. From funds given by the national party to the local branch, the PRG printed propaganda extolling its candidates and maligning the others. The PIACO, with funds from its national organization, printed the same kind of political leaflets, and the PAR was also driven to do so in defense. The week before elections resembled a miniature version of elections in the United States—walls were plastered with leaflets, a sound truck was hired by the PRG and PAR, whispering campaigns impugned the character of the several candidates, and people were exhorted to vote for one or another program.

The PRG did not capture the post of alcalde, but it won three of the four councilmanic seats. The men representing the union were in favor of the municipal government doing everything by law, according to the constitution of the new government. This meant that they urged bypassing the elders in reaching community decisions; nomination for top posts on the basis of party affiliation and party program rather than on age and previous service; and severance from the religious wing of the hierarchy, since they felt that religion should be separate from the state.

The election machinery and party politics were introduced into the Pueblo through the union and its leaders, and this mechanism continued to be the way political leadership was selected until the fall of the Arbenz government in 1954. In the six elections after it first appeared, the PRG continued to challenge the traditional mode of leader selection, group consensus, and public service, and each time more successfully. By 1953–54, during my stay, the PRG had elected the alcalde, the sindico, and three regidores from its ranks. It had ceased to take an active interest in the fate of the cofradías, and one of them folded for lack of personnel. In 1948, the elders had formed the Comité to exert organized pressure upon people to serve in the cofradías, since the civil wing now failed to add its reinforcing sanction and the idea had spread among factory workers that only the civil offices were obligatory. The civil offices were now fair game, and no man selected by traditional criteria stood a chance of assuming one of the six upper offices unless he were also associated with a political party.

There was public disapprobation of this upset in the ordinary course of progress through public office and of the presence of contending factions in the form of political parties, but this was partially offset by the actual achievements of the union men while in office. Through delivering the Cantel vote to the PRG in senatorial elections, they got fulfillment of the promise to build a new rural school. The building was dedicated in 1954, with governor, senator, local party boss, and secretary of education all extolling the tangible benefits of supporting the government and following the lead of the vigorous young men who represented the PRG in Cantel. Contradiction existed between the achievement of ends the community wanted and the means that many saw as irregular or even impious.

In 1954, the union's party won the posts of síndico, the four regidores, and had lost by one vote the post of alcalde. Only 974 votes were cast in this election; five were cast by women, all factory workers. Factory workers were more than proportionately represented, and had a higher percentage of literates voting the PRG ticket. This indicates two things about local politics in Cantel. First, most people will not take sides on a contested issue; they would rather suffer whatever administration comes to power than run the risk of being identified with one of the contestants and thus expose themselves to retribution if their side should lose. Since in Guatemalan politics, both local and national, retribution is exacted by a winner from the loser, this is a reasonable presumption. Second, the organized parties can turn out voters, and they turn out voters who are followers of a personal leader. For example, the 97 voters for the anti-Communist candidate thought he was a good man; there were many more anti-Communists who would not vote for the PIACO candidate because they thought he was a scoundrel. While those in the union who followed the PRG man thought he was personally a very good man, those who did not think so did not participate in the political battle on his behalf. And those campesinos who elected Petronillo as alcalde that year were motivated by the belief that Petronillo's sponsor was a trustworthy man and a fine leader, rather than by the expectation of land grants or rewards from the national government. However, it is true that the PAR did get them a piece of forest land that had long been in dispute with the bordering municipio of Salcajá. (This land later reverted to Salcajá and was always a source of fear for the Cantelenses, since they thought the Salcajeños would make war on Cantel to take back their land—a perfect example of the patria chica notion of the non-national state.)

With the union successful in bringing the legal definition of election and democracy to bear in Cantel and in capturing so many civil posts, the young men decided to go all the way. As the síndico of that year put it to me: "Too long have the old men governed Cantel without knowing how to make a better life. It is time the young men who want everybody to live well, run the municipality." The question of the water supply had come up again, offering an occasion to put this principle into full operation. The municipal corporation decided upon a place from which to pipe water different from that suggested earlier by the principales and the former civil officers. This time they did not even consult the principales but said, in defiance of custom but in accordance with law, "it is the duly elected officers who have the right to say, not the elders." The impact of this breath of the traditional means of group decision was softened by the almost immediate start of the installation of the water system by national engineers. The young union officials' disregard for custom and precedent was again neatly set off by real and visible accomplishment in the material sphere, consequent upon the union's intimate connection with the powers in the capital and the Pueblo's new relation to supralocal power structures via the union.

The State of the Hierarchy

Before the Arbenz government toppled, this was the status of the civil-religious hierarchy:

1. The top offices were filled by election from among candidates proposed by political parties; the PRG, the party of the young union men, was the most successful and was also the initiator and maintainer of this ballot system.

2. The municipal corporation alone reached decisions without the consent of or even consultation with the elders.

3. The civil wing was operating separately from the religious wing; the symbolic links and reinforcing sanctions were absent, making for difficulty in staffing the cofradías.

4. Because the union program had kept the civil and religious wings separate for nearly a decade, many young men coming into civil service had never given religious service.

5. The civil wing of the hierarchy was oriented toward the national government for favors and disposed to implement a program of progress, seen by the union as meaning water, schools, roads, social security, and higher incomes.

6. Prestige was no longer allocated solely by completion of public service in the hierarchy, but could now be gained from connection with the union and a political party.

In brief, the entry of the local union into politics, the control of the election mechanism, the ignoring of principales, the slighting of religious offices, the overriding of the principles of age and public service as criteria for high office and bases of respect, resulted in a civil-religious hierarchy that was badly undermined. This was the major institutional change in Cantel during the entire history of the factory in that community.

The question arises, in my mind, as to what effect this decade of union-youth-politics, backed by the national government, has had on the sentimental structure and value system which supported the old civil-religious hierarchy in its functioning. This is difficult to judge from the evidence I have in hand. Even though the hierarchy was not functioning according to the older pattern and ideal image, it still served as a means of allocating social honor and ordering families in a rank system. At the funerals of past alcaldes of cofradías or their wives, the large turnouts showed the respect and esteem in which these people were held because of the service they had given the Pueblo. I met many people who still thought that the civil-religious hierarchy worked as one system. An extreme instance was the incumbent fiscal of the church, who said that after this post and one more he would be able to retire from the climb up the ladder; to him—he expected to be the next síndico—the two wings were still indistinguishable. When the Arbenz government fell, many people expressed joy over the fact that now there would be no more political parties and that persons qualified in terms of age and experience would again fill the upper posts of the community civil administration. But even as the word of unity and the return to tradition was still warm in the public mouth, the man who took over the post of alcalde was the local leader of PIACO—he took the post and appointed his own party members as regidores. The custom started by the union, that civil office in Cantel was a political thing and was attained by political means, was thus continued. And in the summer of 1956, a political party oriented to Castillo-Armas held all of the top civil posts.

These conflicting kinds of evidence make the regenerative power of the civil-religious hierarchy an open question. I do not think it will ever return to the integral structure it used to be, but rather that it will continue to be secularized and the point of political contention.

LAW AND JUSTICE

While the form and nature of the civil-religious hierarchy was changed during the decade of union activity, its relation to internal canons of law and justice was not. The Cantelense notions of justice and law were met during my stay much as they were in the days of the older informants. This institution was not changed by the factory. Now as then, Cantelenses come to the juzgado, the building where the alcalde dispenses justice; the cases which come before him are the same kind, and about as frequent, as in earlier days. Most disputes are settled in the court of the alcalde. From the case of a son striking a father, or an insult given in the streets, or a drunken husband beating a wife, to the transfer of land and property and the collection of debts, Cantelenses carry their disputes to the impersonal adjudication of the Justice of the Peace. What we would consider an argument to be settled between relatives or amiably adjusted among neighbors, a Cantelense brings into court. The most intimate and personal arguments and difficulties are settled by recourse to law. At law, Cantelenses expect and receive an even-handed dispensation. All know what penalties should be accorded the various crimes and breaches of public order. The hearing is a meeting of the contesting parties to determine on whose side the truth may lie. When a Cantelense says before the alcalde—in sight of the silver-topped cane of office and with one or two of the regidores on hand *čo tioš*, before God— that he is telling the truth, all take his statement to be true. But in most cases I have seen, the point at issue revolves around justification of the action taken, rather than around the question of whether the action was indeed performed as described in the complaint. Justice requires of the alcalde a great ability to sift the stories, to weigh the competing claims, to know the costumbre by which punishment will be meted out, and to convince his hearers that a wise and judicious calculation of the variables has been made in his decision. This is how justice and the notion of law operate in Cantel now and how they operated in the past, so far as one can tell from informants' retrospective judgment of the performance of past alcaldes, which usually turns on the point of how well he handed down wise decisions. The law of the municipio appears then to be an institution that has not been modified through having to deal with factory personnel or factory disputes. Small torts in the factory are treated in the same manner—by the local Justice of the Peace—as are all torts committed in the jurisdiction of the municipality. Local law has never dealt with felonies nor with the legal complications of large landholdings and disputed titles, and it does not do so now. The law and institution of justice was the adjustment of the "tribal" community to the written law of the national entity. It is still that, even though the local community now boasts a specimen of advanced technology.

STATUS AND PRESTIGE

The values and social arrangements connected with honor and respect have not undergone a shift because of the presence of more cash income in the form of factory wages. No one can recall a social class system in the history of Cantel; such differences as there are in power, wealth, prestige, and life style are small and tend to lie between person and person or family and family, rather than between segments of the population collectively distinct from each other in these dimensions. Furthermore, wealth is fluid; the richest man in town worked his way up to that position during his lifetime, while the next richest man inherited wealth from his father. However, the brother of the second richest man, who inherited nearly the same amount of wealth, is well on his way to being a poor man because of excessive drinking. There is no self-perpetuating wealthy class. The 20 or 25 men, depending on the informant, who are called the rich do not found fortunes or pro-create dynasties, for the divisive inheritance process breaks up wealth. The marriage preference of the rich is for poorer mates who will work, and the maintenance of wealth depends upon the continual application of direct labor. Such is still the state of affairs in Cantel.

Prestige is tied to wealth, but not entirely dependent upon it. Almost all men of wealth belong to the category of persons of high social honor and respect. Social honor, in the first instance, comes from having served in the offices of the civil-religious hierarchy. All of the 39 men listed as persons of respect have served in one of the upper posts of either wing of the hierarchy (this is the longest list of wealthy men, and the first 30 persons are nearly identical on similar lists I have collected). Thus, they are all older men. Passing through the offices of the hierarchy requires an outlay of cash and the loss of working time and income; those who have held the top offices have necessarily been those who were able to afford such expenses, or even those who because of wealth or income could pass through the hierarchy most rapidly. The partial coincidence between wealth and prestige is apparent: the wealthier can afford the offices, the older men are usually the wealthier, the wealthier are then those who are older and more accorded social honor.

The ranking of people of respect also depends upon personal behavior. We may here consider status in terms of two components—social honor and social prestige. A man, and by extension his family, accumulates social honor by the discharge of public office; social prestige depends upon his conduct in office and in general social circumstances. Everyone gets deference and honor by having passed through posts in the hierarchy. Prestige is awarded to those who have "behaved well" while in office and who are not "scandalous in the streets." Those whose conduct in office meets the notions of proper behavior, who do not engage in many fights or court cases, who are not drunken and brawling in the streets, are ranked higher than those who have served in similar office but whose general conduct is not so commendable. Upon the balance of these two elements a social status is accorded the individual. The status is validated by formal greetings, by large attendance at funerals in his family, by the invitation to cofradia or civil affairs, and by general knowledge of his prominence.

Power in community affairs was essentially linked to public service and prestige, and ultimately to wealth. But most men expected to exercise such power in the influencing of community decisions and were usually able to, since wealth was not stable, so that a power group of special interest and continuity based on class lines did not, and could not, come into being under the old structure.

There is in the occupational role of workers, and in the slight differences that have come into their lives because of this role, only the dynamic of the union which moves them toward the formation of a new basis for prestige and honor or the formation of classes. The economic advantage of working in the factory is not of such a degree that wealth can be built upon it, nor can factory work change the direct labor basis for the accumulation of wealth.

The political activity of the young union leaders moved the center of power from the principales to political parties but this did not mean the crystallization of a ruling clique, for even the new leaders depended upon mustering a popular vote and hence ultimately on the kind of consensual devices upon which the older power structure rested. The community is not given to a cacique or a class power system, and factory work did not move it in that direction.

THE PASSION PAGEANT

The final institutional setting of factory work which I shall explore is expressed in Easter Week ceremonies. This complex enables me to indicate the nature of cultural and social integration in Cantel, and to show one instance of the amount of conflict this society is able to contain without disruption of social life. I shall briefly describe the events of a part of Easter Week.

Easter Week is the most sacred time of the year. To the Cantelense it is "semana santa" and "semana mayor," holy week and principal week. For the seven weeks preceding it, the community has been building toward the celebration. The trumpeter has been climbing into the bell tower of the church each Friday to send forth his four mournful notes at noon and midnight to portend the tragedy which will be enacted by the Cantelense version of the Passion Play. The players have been rehearsing; the cofrades have been decking the cofradía house floors in pine boughs; the festal foods are being prepared in each household. Arches are built at the principal street crossings and decked with tropical fruits, so that the continual round of sacred processions can wind their way through a town duly adorned. The saints in the church are covered with manta, so that they will not witness the tragic death of the Savior. The huge wooden cross upon which a Cantelense will re-enact the crucifixion is being erected in the plaza. The men who will play the centurions and the people of ancient days are renting their costumes and practicing their dances. The catequistas are putting up pictures of the seven stations to Calvary. The societies of Justo Juez and the Virgen de Soledad and the cofradía of the patron saint are preparing to come out in procession. Everyone in the village is concerned with this holy time in some concrete activity, and the whole atmosphere of the community is charged with the bustle of preparation and permeated with a brooding awareness of the deep sacredness of the events to come.

The chief religious values, and the nature of their integration with the groups which support them, can be seen in the vignette of *Viernes Santo*. Good Friday is to Cantelenses the grandest and most sacred day of the year. This is how Good Friday passes in Cantel. Christ, a Cantelense dressed to resemble the local version of the Lord, is in jail, a room off the plaza turned into a prison for the occasion. He is burdened with the heavy wooden cross and dragged in chains through the streets of Cantel in a faithful reproduction of what is purported to have happened in Jerusalem centuries before. Inside the church, an image of Jesus is hung on a cross to the doleful music of a wailing trumpet and the wild racket of twirling wooden noisemakers, in a moment that is truly climactic as hundreds of Cantelenses file past the crucified image to kneel in saddened homage. The actor has meanwhile been hung up on a crude wooden cross in the plaza and a horseback battle has been enacted between the "Romans" faithful to Christ and those who want him dead.

A procession bearing the image crucified in the church, now laid on a bier, takes to the streets and winds slowly and solemnly into the plaza, where it finds the costumed players of the Passion Play in the midst of judging Judas. At the same time, the local priest with the membership of the Acción Católica de Cantel has entered the plaza to preach on the meaning of the *via crucis*, with the aid of pictures carried by his followers. The scene is striking and goes directly to the core of religious values and symbols in Cantel. About a thousand persons are pressed into the plaza to watch the judging of Judas. The procession enters from one corner and waits until a way is cleared for it to re-enter the church; from the church steps, about seventy people follow the priest and kneel periodically while a catequista explains in Quiché the meaning of each step of the via crucis. The historically separate compartments of the sacred life, the procession and the play, a mixture of Folk Catholicism and pagan elements, are now in one small space, bumping into each other physically but not morally, except in the eyes of the priest. (The Protestants see all three activities as "pagan.") The priest reflects irritation as he is forced to delay his service to allow the procession to pass; he bites his lip as noise from the sentencing of Judas forces him to pause in a prayer; the procession has difficulty threading its way through the throng, and the singing from the Protestant Church down the street is heard when the plaza subsides for a moment. The spectators are dividing their attention between the competing claims from different sectors of the sacred, but paying chief attention to the procession and the show; one or two join the group following the priest and kneel when he prays. The procession enters the church, the priest's group follows, the actors disperse, the Protestants fall silent, and the pageant has come to an end. Tonight people will divide their time between the procession of the sacred interment and the installation in the society of Justo Juez.

This competition between parts of the sacred life is an occasional thing, appearing only in instances where time and personnel must overlap. During most of the year the various elements of the religious institutions function without conflict or friction, and people do not act or feel in terms of my analytical categories of organized Christian, Folk Catholicism, and esoteric religious experience. The disharmony arising from the competing values and conflicting groups in the religious sphere does not seem to arouse disharmony in the individual. They take it that all these expressions of devotion and symbols of sacredness have equal validity and an equal claim to support. The institutional structure of Cantel contains conflicting elements which arouse no desire to straighten them out and bring them into line along one axis. The parts of the social system are linked together loosely; the nature of cultural integration in this community is such that contrasting and even conflicting values and norms coexist, and the occasional conflict does not bring them into closer consistency. The cultural integration of Cantel is not a fine web in which pulling on one thread throws the whole design out of balance.

It is into this kind of institutional structure and setting that the factory was introduced and has continued to prosper. Viewed in this way, the factory is another square added to the cultural mesh of Cantel.

OCCUPATIONAL ASPIRATIONS

One further word needs to be said about current values in connection with operation of the factory. Has the factory developed in the future working population a set of occupational aspirations in line with its use of manpower? We asked 136 school children (91 boys and 45 girls all between 10 and 15 years of age) in grades 2 to 5 in the factory and Pueblo schools about job preferences. It appears that occupational aspirations only imperfectly reflect the fact that there is a factory in Cantel. The predominant choice of both boys and girls is to be in a special occupation (artisan, merchant, etc.). Factory work accounted for 18 percent of the choice of Indian girls, and 18.7 percent of Indian boys. However, the number of boys aspiring to be mechanics and tailors, and girls to be seamstresses, far exceeds the foreseeable local demand for such services.

Only 23.1 percent of the boys interviewed wanted to follow the same occupation as their fathers, and most of those had artisan fathers. The important observation is that the occupational pre-ferences of young Cantelenses are not oriented toward the two major uses of manpower in this community—farm and factory—but rather toward the artisans and self-employed status. The oft expressed regard for farm work is not reflected in the younger generation's hopes and desires about occupations. The operation of the factory for seventy years has not created a proletarian view of job opportunities—a view that factory work is inevitable. Since our sample came from children in school, it may reflect the role of the school in fostering social mobility drives and in widening the horizon of jobs desired.

The older values of independence and self-sufficiency, expressed by the mature in terms of land-holding, have come to be seen by the young in terms of skilled or semiskilled artisan jobs or small shops or businesses.

These differences between generations can also be seen by a glance at the occupational aspirations of Indian men in night school classes. Of the 19 men taking these classes, 10 expressed no desire to change their occupations as a result of the skills they learned in night school. The older generation appears so tied to the community by economic fitness, social obligation, and personal identity that it cannot afford to aspire to the artisan or semiskilled job, with its partial threat of having to move from the local society.

10

Conclusions

CANTEL is not the same society it was before the introduction of the factory. But it is still a going concern and still a distinct way of life, rich in local meanings and in patterns of social relations far removed from the kinds of societies which have invented and spread machine technology. Cantel's experience with the mechanisms of adjustment to a new economic form and its resultant pressures means at least this: factories may be introduced into peasant societies without the drastic chain of social, cultural, and psychological consequences implied in the concept of "revolution." The idea that social change involving new forms of production is necessarily wasteful in human terms finds no support in Cantel.

To judge from Cantel, a people's ability to accommodate to new cultural forms is intimately related to their actual and felt control over their social circumstances. The sense of control seems to stem from their freedom to choose how they will combine the new elements, and to discard or accept the innovations as their consequences become clear. Cantelenses did not begin to absorb the factory into their communal life until force and the threats of force were withdrawn. They began to come to the factory as workers when they realized it as a means of implementing some of their goals.

Cantelenses, like others, have a way of life that is infinitely perfectible, and they are willing to experiment, to make choices, to try new things—but in a situation where they feel able to make the social decisions as to what ends shall be sought. They are often mistaken as to the consequences of social decisions; they often try to balance incompatibles, or to pursue contradictory and mutually exclusive ends. For, like us, they discover what they want in the act of daily living—in the business of trying to balance the elements of culture and personal situation so that a society emerges which they find worth living in.

Social scientists are not in an empirically strong position when they attempt to predict what aspects of social life will be contradictory or mutually exclusive. Theoretical expectations, the reported facts on the impact of factories in non-Western societies, the run of historical experience, all pointed to a situation that should have worked out differently than the one I found in Cantel. I did not expect that industry could operate effectively in a social setting so different from a Western social structure. I think it is manifest that the range of cultural understanding and social structure in which factories may operate is not yet charted. We have much more to learn before we lay down the range of alternatives open to a society in the process of technological and economic change.

I do not mean to imply a "universe with the lid off" where any kind of productive system and any kind of institutional setting may coexist. Nor do I mean to convey the impression that the introduction and operation of an industrial technology can always be relatively painless in preindustrial or nonindustrial societies.

Cantel presents something of an exception in terms of contemporary experience with the diffusion of industrial technology, or when viewed against the historical evolution of industrial society.

From the perspective of the shattering experiences of contemporary industrialization in the non-Western world or the English experience in the 18th century, the special characteristics of Cantel culture and social circumstance which have permitted its accommodation to industrial production are highlighted. The comparisons also enable us to say with some confidence what may be attributed to the operation of a factory as such, as against those conditions which are putatively necessary to the indigenous development of industrial production.

Elsewhere I have surveyed the effects of village industrialization on South and East Asia (Nash 1955b). Social disruption and cultural disintegration have been regular concomitants of industrial production in that part of the world, but the sources of social stress cannot be ascribed to the factory as such. In China, for example, the political and ideological changes and the urban-bred notions of personal relations which have accompanied the establishment of industrial enterprise in peasant villages have been the chief solvents on peasant life, not the factory. Cantel made its greatest changes during a revolutionary decade, but it never surrendered control of its affairs to a central government. The most revolutionary of ideas and activities can be handled by a small society like Cantel if local people, without absolute political and economic power, are the agents and adherents of the new ways. Cantel worked out its adjustment to an influx of new ideas in an arena where local people could make the ultimate choice. Unlike China, the factory was not the government, and the government was not specifically committed to the success of the factory.

In Africa, where the effects of industrialization upon tribal peoples have been especially marked, special circumstances attend the disruptions. In most of Africa, money wages and industrial work have been accompanied by the separation of the wage worker from his village, with his consequent removal from the sanctions and social controls of the tribal society. When people are removed from a set of social relations and placed in a work situation where satisfying new ones are not permitted to emerge, the kinds of changes summarized by Mair (1953; 1–171) may be routinely anticipated.

Moore (1955: 41), relying upon extensive surveys of published material on contemporary industrialization (Moore 1951, 1948a, 1948b), holds that:

To the question of the impact of industry on the structure of society at least partial answers are available. Industrialization involves urbanization in some degree, and is uniformly destructive of extended kinship systems (where binding mutual obligations prevail among many relatives of various degrees), and traditional modes of social stratification. In one way or another, all of these consequences are linked to the industrialization process by the *mobility* required by the latter.

Cantel conforms in part with this diagnosis. But the positive side of the orderly emergence of new modes of stratification, and the deeper if not wider integration of family life, are not noted in Moore's conclusions. I am not so much interested in what has to be sacrificed in industrialization as in what can be gained. Cantel indicates that many areas of traditional life can flourish on a new level in the process of industrialization, and that the release of human energy and creative ability in a process of social change can devise solutions to problems of social life—solutions not prefigured in our theory or achieved in other instances of similar change.

The analysis of historical experience, at least in England, poses a slightly different set of questions than those posed by the spread of an already established technology. The theoretical nature of the development of an industrial society is beginning to be understood. The question of how a society may totally reorient its social structure and culture pattern so that it may generate continual economic progress, obviously requires greater changes than have taken place in Cantel, changes probably of the order suggested by Hoselitz (1953).

In 18th-century England, a whole social structure was transformed by technological advance and the ascendancy of a new social class. Plumb (1950) indicates the effects this social transformation had on the local villages, making the worker an adjunct to the productive process and denying him the customary protection against want. In their famous work on the village laborer, the Hammonds (1948) have indicated the effects of the corn laws, the uprooting of the villager from his traditional place, the use of industrial technology as a source of social power above and beyond the end of increased production. George (1953) describes the changes in mid-18th century village life in the wake of the rise of a new political class, and the consequent hardships upon factory workers. These writers stress the changing moral, political, and military climate that accompanied the industrialization of mercantile England. An extended survey of historical experience is beyond my competence and the needs of this work. What this brief selection means to convey is that in addition to the revolution in productive process and technology, there was a social upheaval in the displacement of farmers and artisans and their transformation into a depressed proletariat, while a new social class of entrepreneurs rose to positions of social and economic power and prestige.

Against this background of contemporary experience and historical evolution of industrialization, the more general factors accounting for Cantel's smooth accommodation to factory production may be explored. Some novelty attaches to Cantel's experience. It is an instance where *only* factory production was added to the community, unaccompanied by the simultaneous advent of democratic notions of political and social organization (except for the last decade of revolt). By the time that the 1944 revolution suddenly widened the channels of communication between Cantel and the nation and poured new notions of social life down those channels, Cantel had absorbed the factory. Its response to the revolutionary decade was based on the fact that it was in part a factory community. Cantel's closer allegiance to the national government, its turn from age to youth in leadership patterns, and the breakup of the civil-religious hierarchy, could not have come had there not been a social basis in the factory worker's union.

But these changes, like the factory itself, came into a community in which there had been ethnic continuity. People who were to work in the factory or join the new political parties had already worked out a set of social understandings and personal relationships prior to the factory or the revolution. The physical sameness of the population meant that no imported and alien population or cultural tradition came into the local society to compete with and perhaps undermine it.

A second factor was that organization of risk connected with the operation of the economic firm was carried on beyond the bounds of the local society. The local society was not concerned with these special devices and social arrangements necessary to the operation of a firm facing a market where continued existence may depend upon the fineness of calculation and maximization of production. The local people did not have to develop ways of dealing with them. And the factory, perhaps due to its semimonopolistic position, was able to give steady and continuous employment; the local people were not subject to the boom-and-bust cycle of factory employment in an uncertain market.

Third, there was no effective transfer of the means of social coercion to persons outside the local society. And no new social class arose in Cantel. Since outsiders did not possess the power to make the Cantel factory worker an adjunct to the private search for profit or the statistical cog in some giant plan for rapid economic advance, the old social system continued to be the chief means of prestige and social control. A new social class did not try to make Cantel into its image, nor could supralocal persons treat the Cantelenses as so many economic units of manpower.

Fourth, the new industry did not compete with established ways of making a living. Artisan production and farm work were not undercut by removal of a significant part of the labor force. In Cantel, the common features of economic depression, due to the shriveling of native production, and economic boom, due to the introduction of new ways of production, did not occur.

Fifth, the culture and social structure of Cantel contained

many elements favorable to factory work and industrialization. Cantelenses were peasants, already used to money exchange, familiar with the estimation of economic advantage, at ease with impersonal economic relations. Conditions of work prior to the factory stressed discipline, time calculation, continuous physical effort, and regular work habits. There were no large clans or lineages to be subverted. The values of the community were those of industry, thrift, and work, and wealth was considered good. The culture was a receptive one, which for centuries had been selectively incorporating elements from the national Guatemalan culture and world society. This kind of society, with this cultural integration, appears especially propitious for the relatively smooth accommodation to industrial work.

These factors are put forth as the social conditions and cultural background against which "easy" industrialization may take place. The larger generalization, then, is that there are kinds of societies and cultures which under special social circumstances may accommodate with relative smoothness to industrial production. I see the following implications for both theory and practice in this generalization:

A theory of social and cultural change capable of dealing with the consequences of social decisions in situations of uncertain outcome is yet to be fashioned. I believe change is best understood as the result of the ways in which individuals choose to combine time, effort, and resources in the face of new opportunity. These factors, in their purposeful combination, underlie the emergence of new social relations and cultural understandings.

As these and similar ideas are elaborated by further research, a theory of change will emerge in which the role of choice will be analytically coordinate with the characteristics of the social and cultural systems. In fact, I envision an approach which deals with social systems as conditioning choice in two ways: (1) by generating sets of alternatives, and (2) by defining the means by which alternatives may be implemented. My study of Cantel is one attempt to further this theoretical development.

Although a theory of change adequate to contemporary problems is not complete, the main procedural and practical lines of effecting change are indicated on the basis of current knowledge.

Chiefly, I should like to say this to those interested in minimizing the human costs of technological advance. First, discard the ideal that there are specific answers as yet. At best we are equipped with diagnostic tools, which enable us to point to the situations where most stress and strain may be generated. Second, a program which is highly flexible, permitting members of the society undergoing change to choose freely and discard easily from the alternatives offered them, is most likely to be effective. Third, when the end is technological and economic development, the largest problem in social change is the task of enlisting the energies and sentiments of the people involved, not the communication of expert knowledge to the benighted.

If the administrator or technical expert assumes a tentative attitude toward the best means of social change, and if he spends the better part of his energies in the clarification of alternatives in a situation of relatively unhampered choice, he maximizes the possibilities of successful change. No amount of general knowledge can ever substitute for detailed knowledge of the particular circumstances of change, or for the art of foreseeing consequences which might become social tragedies.

Cantel teaches the general lesson that the human tolls in industrialization are not built into the process itself. They are the result of an image of man in social change which delineates him as the passive agent mechanically responding to immutable forces, or as the pawn in a political chess game, or as the expendable material in an economic vision. The questions we must ask of the process of industrialization cannot be phrased apart from the ineluctable fact that man makes himself, or he is not made at all.

References Cited

DIRECCIÓN GENERAL DE ESTADÍSTICA
 1924   Quarto Censo de la Población de la Republica, 1921.
         Guatemala City.
 1950   Sexto Censo de Población. Guatemala City.
EGGAN, FRED
 1954   Social anthropology and the method of controlled comparison. American Anthropologist 56:743–63.
FIRTH, RAYMOND
 1953   Elements of social organization. New York, Philosophical Library.
GEORGE, DOROTHY
 1953   England in transition. Suffolk, Penguin Books.
GILLIN, JOHN
 1945   Parallel cultures and the inhibitions to acculturation in a Guatemalan community. Social Forces 24:1–14.
GOUBAUD, ANTONIO C.
 1952   Indian adjustments to modern national culture. *In* Acculturation in the Americas, Sol Tax ed. Chicago, University of Chicago Press.
HAMMOND, J. L. AND BARBARA
 1948   The village labourer. I & II. London, Guild Books.
HOSELITZ, BERT F.
 1953   Social structure and economic growth. Economia Internazionale 6:4–28.
LA FARGE, OLIVER
 1940   Maya ethnology: the sequence of cultures. *In* The Maya and their neighbors. New York, D. Appleton-Century.
LEWIS, OSCAR
 1951   Life in a Mexican village: Tepoztlán restudied. Urbana University of Illinois Press.

MAIR, L. P.

1953   African marriage and social change. *In* Survey of African marriage and family life, Arthur Phillips ed. London, International African Institute.

MCBRYDE, FELIX WEBSTER

1945   Cultural and historical geography of Southwest Guatemala. Smithsonian Institute of Social Anthropology No. 4. Washington, D. C.

MOORE, WILBERT E.

1948a   Primitives and peasants in industry. Social Research 15:41–81.

1948b   Theoretical aspects of industrialization. Social Research 15:277–303.

1951   Industrialization and labor. Ithaca, Cornell University Press.

1955   Economy and society. New York, Doubleday & Co.

NASH, MANNING

1955a   The reaction of a civil-religious hierarchy to a factory in Guatemala. Human Organization 13:26–28.

1955b   Some notes on village industrialization in South and East Asia. Economic Development and Cultural Change 3:271–77.

1956a   Recruitment of wage labor and the development of new skills. Annals of the American Academy of Political and Social Science 305:23–32.

1956b   Relaciones Políticas en Guatemala. *In* Integración social en Guatemala. Seminario de Integración Social, Guatemala City.

PLUMB, J. H.

1950   England in the eighteenth century (1714–1815). Penguin Books. London.

REDFIELD, ROBERT AND SOL TAX

1952   General characteristics of present day Mesoamerican Indian Society. *In* Heritage of conquest, Sol Tax ed. Glencoe, Illinois, Free Press.

TAX, SOL

1937   The municipios of the Midwestern Highlands of Guatemala. American Anthropologist 39:423–44.

1941   World view and social relations in Guatemala. American Anthropologist 43:27–42.

1953   Penny capitalism: a Guatemalan Indian economy.

Smithsonian Institute of Social Anthropology, No. 16. Washington, D. C.

WAGLEY, CHARLES

1941   Economics of a Guatemalan village. Memoirs of the American Anthropological Association 58.

1949   The social and religious life of a Guatemalan village. Memoirs of the American Anthropological Association 71.

WALLACE, ANTHONY F. C.

1952   The modal personality structure of the Tuscarora Indians. Bureau of American Ethnology Bulletin 150. Washington, D. C.

Index